Learning to Ride

Learning to Ride

Jane Kidd
Consulting Editor

HOWELL BOOK HOUSE
New York

Maxwell Macmillan Canada
Toronto

Maxwell Macmillan International
New York Oxford Singapore Sydney

Howell Book House
Macmillan Publishing Company
866 Third Avenue
New York, NY 10022

Maxwell Macmillan Canada, Inc.
1200 Eglinton Avenue East, Suite 200
Don Mills, Ontario M3C 3NI

Macmillan Publishing Company is part of the Maxwell Communication Group of Companies.

Library of Congress Cataloging-in-Publication Data
Learning to ride/consulting editor, Jane Kidd.
p. cm.
Includes index.
Summary: Illustrations and text provide information on such aspects of English-style horseback riding as basic paces, jumping, rider form, schooling a horse, and working over different terrains.
ISBN 0-87605-961-2
1. Horsemanship-Juvenile literature. [1. Horsemanship.]
I. Kidd, Jane.
SF309.2.L43 1993
798.2—dc20   92—15100   CIP   AC

Macmillan books are available at special discounts for bulk purchases for sales promotions, premiums, fund-raising, or educational use. For details, contact:

Special Sales Director
Macmillan Publishing Company
866 Third Avenue
New York, NY 10022

10 9 8 7 6 5 4 3 2 1

Printed in Hong Kong

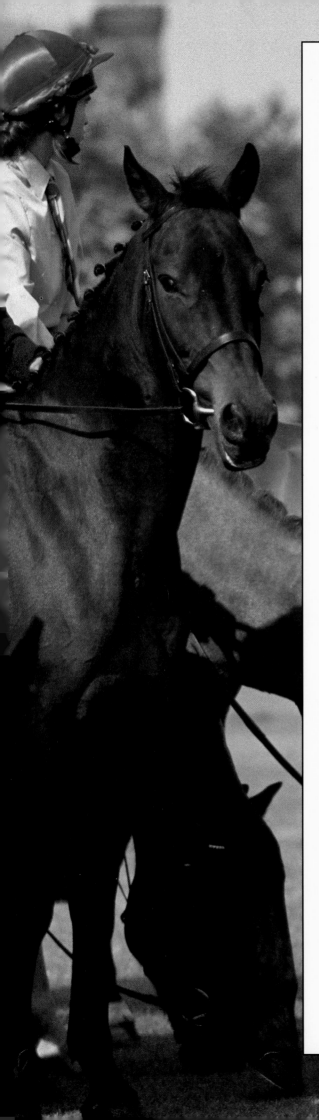

Contents

1 First lessons

Your first lesson

When you first decide to take up riding, you'll have to think about all sorts of things like who's going to teach you, what you should wear and what you can do in advance to get the most out of your lessons.

Choosing a school

As a starting point, take time to find a good teacher. Not everyone who can *ride* well is expert at helping someone else to learn, so it's usually better to go to an established riding school rather than asking a friend for help.

Get advice from anyone you know who rides regularly or look through local telephone directories and newspapers for the names and addresses of stables. You can then visit the schools to see which you like best.

Having chosen a school, book a short lesson to begin with. Half an hour is about right as you may be surprised at how tired you get. Later, you can book longer sessions. It's also better to book lessons close together – with no more than a week between each one. Otherwise, it's difficult to remember what you've been taught.

What to wear

For your first lesson, you shouldn't have to buy any special kit but check that your chosen school can provide you with a proper riding hat. *Never* go riding without one. Sturdy shoes with smooth soles (so they don't get caught in the stirrups), a pair of well-fitting jeans and a comfortable top are the only other requirements.

▼ **When you meet** the pony you are going to ride, spend some time making friends with him: talk to him and pat him so he feels he knows you.

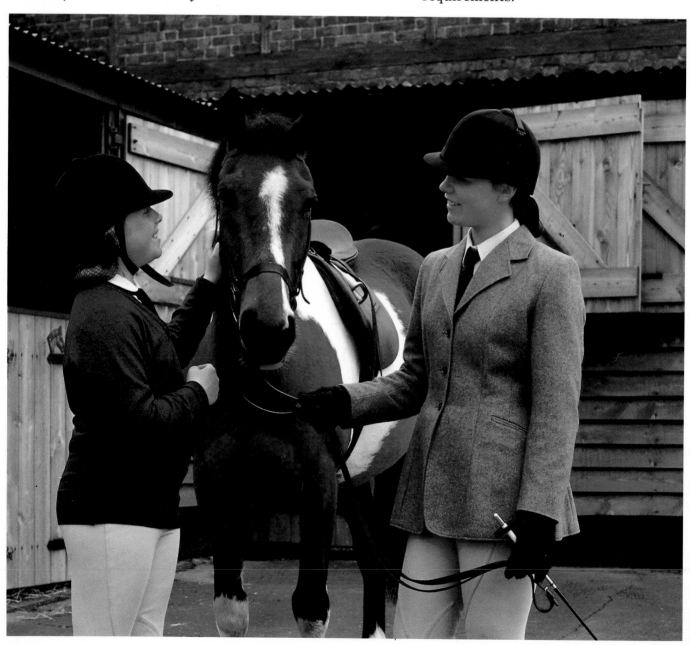

How to prepare

Before you go for your lesson, aim to read up about riding and horse care. Get to know some of the names given to different parts of the saddle and bridle – the reins, girth and so on – and look at people on horseback to see how they sit and what they do.

It's also helpful to learn a few of the names for different parts of the horse: you don't have to memorize everything at once – just try to remember a few new details each week.

The lesson

When you start, you will be given a steady, reliable pony. Ask what his name is and, when he is led out of his stable, talk to him and stroke him. Your teacher will help you and tell you what

to do, so just relax and enjoy your first meeting!

The pony will already be tacked-up (with his saddle and bridle on) and you'll have time to look at the way everything 'fits together'. The saddle is carefully designed to make riding more comfortable for you and to make sure that your weight is evenly spread across the pony's back. The reins are linked to a bit (a metal bar which rests in the horse's mouth) and they are for telling the pony to turn or to stop.

Mounting

The first thing you'll be taught is how to get on the pony. Stand to the side of the pony, with your left shoulder to his. By facing the tail as you put your foot in the stirrups, you don't get left behind if ►

DID YOU KNOW?
The toe stirrup – a loop of rope just large enough to hold the rider's big toe – was once widely used in the East. It is still popular in Southern India, Singapore and Malaya.

How to mount

1 Stand on the left side of the pony, facing the tail. Gather the reins loosely in your left hand and grasp a good tuft of mane.

2 With your right hand, turn the stirrup iron outward to face you, and put your left foot into it. If it's a bit high for you, the instructor can lengthen the stirrup leather.

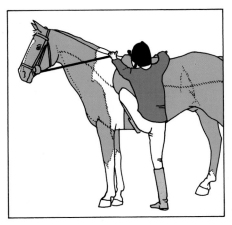

3 Put your right hand on the far side of the saddle, and your weight on the stirrup iron, placing your toe under the pony's tummy. Spring off your right foot to face the pony's side.

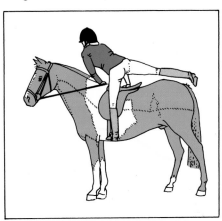

4 Swing your leg over the pony's back and lower yourself gently into the saddle. Put your right foot in the right stirrup iron – at first you'll have to guide your foot in.

MISTAKES!

Don't dig the pony in the ribs as you mount. He'll find it uncomfortable and may take it as a signal to move off before you are ready.

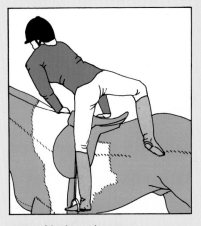

Avoid kicking the pony as you swing your leg over his back. It may make him start forward or even buck.

the pony walks forward. In any case, first time around the instructor will probably hold the reins near the bridle to stop the pony moving off. Although later on you'll need to hold the reins tightly enough to control the pony, for the moment just gather them up loosely in your left hand.

With your other hand, turn the stirrup iron outwards, and put your left foot into it. If it's a bit high, the stirrup leather can be lengthened.

Gently does it

Grasp the back of the saddle with your right hand and put your weight on the stirrup iron, pressing your toe under the pony's middle – don't give him a dig in the ribs! Spring up facing the pony's side. To start with, the instructor can hold down the stirrup iron on the other side so that the saddle doesn't slip.

Swing your leg over the pony's back and sit down lightly on the saddle. Try not to thump down like a sack of potatoes or you'll give him an unpleasant jolt. Put your right foot in the right stirrup iron – at the beginning you'll have to look down to do this.

How to sit

Although you may find it strange at first, you'll soon get used to sitting on a pony. Your 'seat' position is very important as it helps you to stay comfortable and safe when you ride. Concentrate on getting a good seat now and you'll be a much better rider in the future.

Sit upright, with your seat bones firmly in the middle of the saddle. Keep your back straight, hold your head up and look forward.

Rest your thighs and knees against each side of the pony so that your weight is evenly balanced and you don't tip one way or the other. Stay relaxed: if you grip tightly with your legs, you'll push yourself up and out of the saddle.

Put the ball of your foot in the stirrups, toes up and your heel down. Try to keep your toes pointing forward – not sticking out like butterfly wings!

Once you've settled and think you are sitting correctly, try to imagine a line drawn through the middle of your head and going straight down, through your shoulder, then your hip and finishing on your heel. If that line has to bend or turn sharply, then something is wrong with your seat.

THE CORRECT SEAT

A 'good seat' is the aim of every rider, so practise sitting properly from your first lesson.

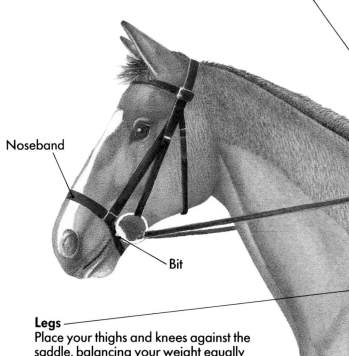

Hands
At the beginning, gather the reins loosely; if you feel at all insecure, grasp the mane or hold on to the pommel.

Noseband

Bit

Legs
Place your thighs and knees against the saddle, balancing your weight equally on either side. Just rest your legs – don't grip or you'll push yourself upwards out of the saddle and spoil your position.

Feet
Put the ball of your foot in the stirrup irons and push your toes up – then your heel will automatically go down and your ankle bend. Make sure your toes point forward, not out, so you avoid squeezing the pony's side with your heels making him move off.

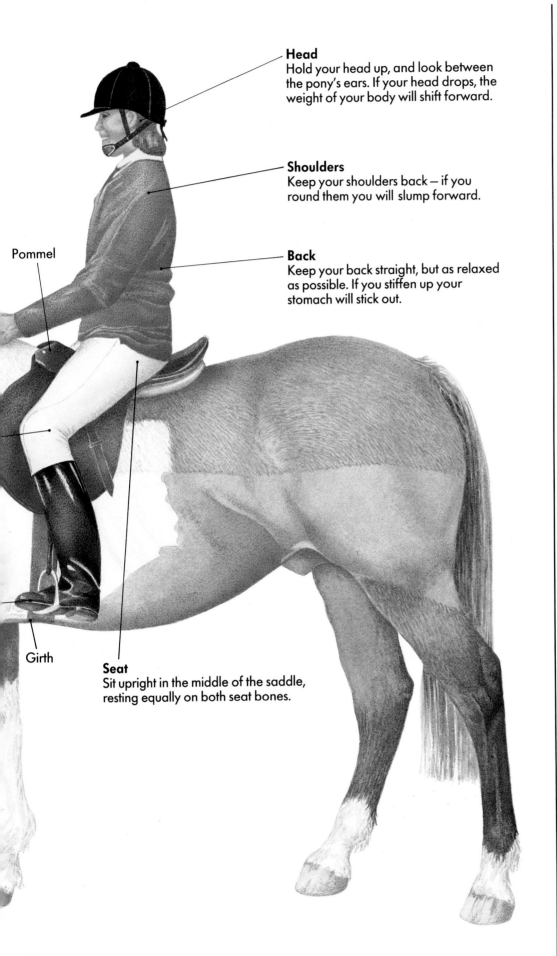

Head
Hold your head up, and look between the pony's ears. If your head drops, the weight of your body will shift forward.

Shoulders
Keep your shoulders back — if you round them you will slump forward.

Pommel

Back
Keep your back straight, but as relaxed as possible. If you stiffen up your stomach will stick out.

Girth

Seat
Sit upright in the middle of the saddle, resting equally on both seat bones.

❗ SAFETY NET
● If you have long hair, it's best to get into the habit of wearing a rider's hairnet. Loose hair can get caught in low branches, or obscure your view.
   Not only is loose hair a safety hazard, but any faults in your position are emphasized if your hair flies about all over the place as you ride.

Know your paces

The walk

The walk is a regular four-time movement and the horse always has two or three hooves on the ground.

The horse lifts his hooves as follows: foreleg (1), diagonal hindleg (2), other foreleg (3), remaining hindleg (4).

By following the numbered red hooves you can count the beat of each pace.

The trot

The trot is a steady two-time action. The horse moves opposite diagonal legs together, changing from one pair to the other with a moment in between when all four legs are off the ground — eg, right fore and left hind (1), then left fore and right hind (2).

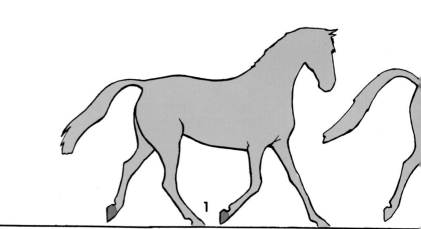

The canter

The canter is a three-time movement.

The sequence for the canter is: either hindleg lifting (1), the other hindleg and its diagonal foreleg together (2), the remaining foreleg (3). Finally, there is a moment when all four legs are in mid-air.

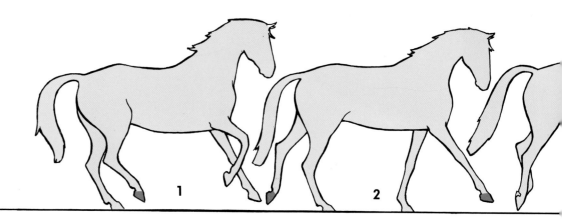

The gallop

The gallop is a variation of the canter, but the legs move one at a time. It is a four-time action.

There are two gallop sequences — either hindleg lifts (1), followed by the other hindleg (2), its diagonal foreleg (3) and then the remaining foreleg (4).

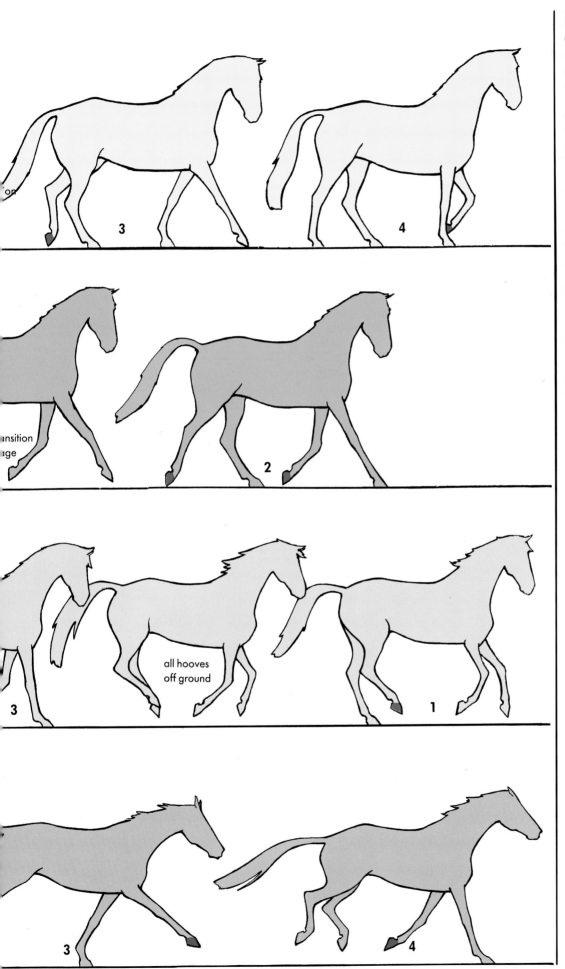

3

4

ansition
ge

2

all hooves
off ground

3

1

3

4

Riding each pace

Understanding how the horse moves helps you to ride correctly.

Most horses have three basic paces: the walk, the trot and the canter, with its faster version, the gallop.

The pattern of movement is different at each pace but with practice you can ride them all smoothly.

The walk is the steadiest and most comfortable pace.

The trot has two beats to every pace and a moment in mid-air, so it's more comfortable for the rider (and the horse) to rise up and down in time with the rhythm.

To do the rising trot, let your horse's stride push you up from the saddle and then lower you down gently in an even movement.

The canter is a bounding movement which is quite jerky and tiring for the rider. Practise in short bursts at first. Unlike the trot, keep your seat in the saddle.

The gallop is the fastest pace of all. To increase their speed, horses take longer strides. They push harder and their hooves stay on the ground for less time.

To help the flow of the horse's movement, lift your seat slightly out of the saddle, putting your weight on your knees and feet. But before galloping, make sure you can control your horse at a canter.

Starting and walking

Once you are sitting correctly in the saddle, you're ready to start walking. So you need to know how to tell the pony to move off and how to adjust your position to the pony's movement.

Check your position

From the beginning, develop the habit of being able to check your own position. Hold the pommel with both hands and pull yourself down into the saddle. This helps you to sit really deeply. Then ask yourself a few questions.

Balance

Do you feel balanced, sitting evenly on both your seat bones and are your stirrups of equal and comfortable length? Is your upper body upright, but relaxed? If you sit up straight your shoulders will fall into the correct position.

Are you looking straight ahead between the pony's ears or slightly above them? Never look down. Your head is surprisingly heavy. If it droops, or you move it in the wrong direction, your balance can be badly affected. Gazing at the ground is a common mistake, seen at all levels of riding, but if you never start you won't have to learn to stop!

Your legs

Are your calves still back and underneath you, with your knees slightly bent? If you glance down you should only just be able to see the tips of your toes peeping out from underneath your knees.

Think about lowering the heel and raising the toe, without straining your ankle. It takes a lot of practice before your muscles learn to work in this way.

Leading rein and lunge rein

Depending on your riding school, your early lessons will probably take place either on the lunge rein, or on the leading rein.

On the lunge, the instructor controls

CAVESSON
A lungeing cavesson has three rings on the noseband. These are for the lunge rein and side-reins.

► **Having a lesson** on the lunge rein means you can concentrate on sitting correctly while someone else controls the pony using a lungeing whip. Long enough to reach the horse and so guide him round in a circle, it measures at least 165cm (66in).

14

the pony by a lunge line (a long rein) which is attached to a special noseband called the lunge cavesson. The pony moves in a large circle.

On the leading rein, an assistant leads the pony (either from the ground or from another horse) by holding a rope attached to the bridle.

Whichever method your riding school uses, the pony is under the control of the instructor or helper for these early lessons. You don't have to think about controlling the pony, so you can concentrate on your position and your balance, and get used to the feel of the pony.

Forward to walk

As you prepare to move forward to walk put your hands on the pommel (the front of the saddle) or hold on to a neck strap (usually a stirrup leather buckled around the pony's neck). Until you are more familiar with the technique for walking, don't do more than gather the reins loosely.

Stay relaxed and keep breathing! It sounds silly, but it is amazing how everyone holds their breath when concentrating hard on something. Make sure that no part of your body is tense, or you will pass your anxiety on to the pony.

Try to keep your position and think of the straight line: Ear – Shoulder – Hip – Heel. It's all too easy to tip forward or to be left behind. Do this before going from the halt to walk.

Any change of pace like this is called a transition, and whether it's faster or slower, the rider should always think 'forward'.

To walk on, squeeze the pony's sides with your lower leg, pressing and releasing until he responds by stepping forward. Once the pony is walking, keep a *slight* pressure with the legs. Don't clamp them to the pony's sides or take them away completely.

Concentrate on maintaining a safe seat and stay relaxed. Enjoy yourself!

★ SIDE REINS

These may be attached to the cavesson. They can be bought specially, or the instructor can use the reins, unbuckled in the middle and tied to the cavesson and girth.

Side-reins encourage the pony to keep a correct head position, and mean that he doesn't start grazing or throwing his head up. And, as long as they are the same length, they stop him bending more to one side than the other.

Exercises in the saddle

At any level, exercises in the saddle help to develop your balance and confidence on the pony. Riding can be very tiring and your muscles can start to ache after only 30 minutes. The more used to the basic riding movements your muscles become, the less stiff you'll be.

It's possible to exercise at home if you don't have your own pony. Stand with your feet placed about 60cm (2ft) apart. Keep your upper body straight but not stiff. Then just bend at the knee slightly, as though you were sitting on a pony. There you are, in position for riding! Bounce a little at the knee, straightening and bending. Do some of the arm exercises here as well and you'll soon be supple.

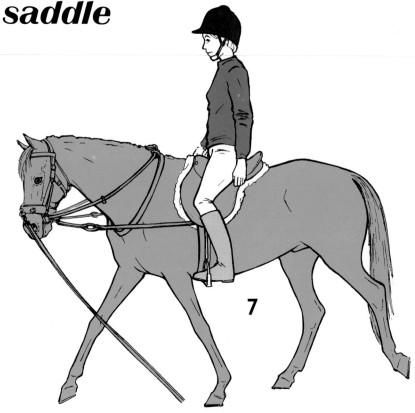

7 **Lifting leg (continued)**
. . . release your leg and, without looking, let it drop down so that it falls more naturally into the correct riding position. Repeat this exercise four or five times with both legs.

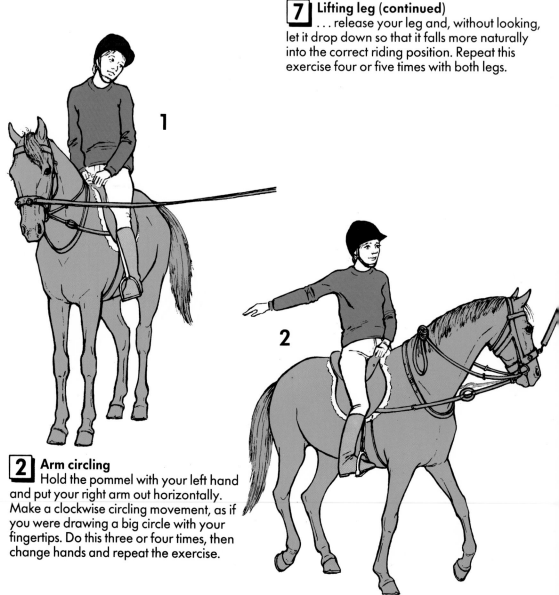

1 **Head turning**
With your horse at the halt, hold on to the pommel with one or both hands. Slowly move your head ten times as if your nose was drawing a figure of eight. This relaxes your neck muscles.

2 **Arm circling**
Hold the pommel with your left hand and put your right arm out horizontally. Make a clockwise circling movement, as if you were drawing a big circle with your fingertips. Do this three or four times, then change hands and repeat the exercise.

5 **Bending forward**
Sit upright and put your hands on your hips. Bend forward, as far as you can without tipping over. If you feel unsafe to begin with, do this exercise with one hand on the pommel. Repeat five times to strengthen your stomach muscles.

5

6

6 **Lifting leg**
Put your right hand on the pommel. With your left hand lift your left leg as far back and up as it will go. Hold it there for a second or two . . .

4

3 **Punching the air**
Holding on to the pommel with one hand, punch the air in all directions with your other hand. This loosens your shoulder and back muscles. Repeat the exercise six times with each arm.

3

4 **Body twists**
Stretch both arms out to the sides, at shoulder height. From the waist, turn to your left. Push your left arm as far round to the left as you can. Do this several times with both arms. Body twists are especially good for your balance, and for making your waist supple.

Adjusting the tack

When you're used to the feel of sitting on a pony, you're ready to learn how to adjust the tack so both you and your pony are comfortable and safe.

The girth

The girth is the strap that runs under the pony's middle and keeps the saddle fastened on. It must be secure without being tight. If it is too loose, the saddle slips round as you mount or when the pony starts moving.

A girth that is too tight is safer – but it's uncomfortable for the pony. The girth straps can pinch him, particularly

if his skin gets wrinkled and caught underneath. This may irritate the pony, and make him more likely to play up, ignoring your commands.

Checking and adjusting

The girth needs to be checked before you get on and after you have been riding for about ten minutes.

When you start riding, your instructor will probably check the girth for you before you mount the pony. But you should know how to adjust it yourself. Loosely holding the reins, slide your hand flat under the girth. If your fingers

▼ **Once you've fastened** the girth securely, you can begin to enjoy the lesson!

18

fit snugly, the girth is correctly fastened; if not the buckles can be tightened or loosened accordingly.

You should also learn to check the girth when you're in the saddle. After you've been riding for a short time, the girth needs to be checked again because the pony has warmed up and the saddle may have worked loose. If you think the girth does need tightening, shift your leg in front of the saddle. Keep your foot in the stirrup iron. Lift the saddle flap, pull the girth strap up and tighten the buckle a couple of notches.

Eventually, you'll be able to manage it looking ahead and while the pony walks on. To start with, practise with someone holding the pony while you look down and see what you're doing.

Pony tricks

Some mischievous ponies enjoy blowing themselves out as you do the girth up. When you mount, or after a few minutes of riding, they breathe out so that the saddle slips round and you end up under the pony's middle.

Take extra care to check the girth if you ride a pony like this so you don't get caught out by tricks!

Checking the girth

◄ **Before you mount,** check the girth by placing your fingers flat under it once the saddle is secured to the pony. Extra space or wrinkled flesh mean it is either too loose or too tight!

If it does need tightening, lift the saddle flap (the leather flap that your leg rests against when riding) and pull up the girth strap. Fasten the buckle a hole or two higher and run your fingers underneath the girth to make sure that no skin is caught.

◄ **After about ten minutes** of riding, check the girth again. If it has worked loose, move your leg forward – with your foot still in the stirrup iron – so that it rests in front of the saddle. Lift the saddle flap and tighten the girth strap one or two holes as shown in the detail below.

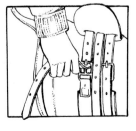

★ **NEAR AND OFF**

The terms *near* and *off* are often used when talking about horses. *Near* refers to the left of the pony and *off* to the right.

Most ponies are used to being handled on the near side – this is the side you've learnt to mount from.

It might be confusing at first, but it's well worth memorizing these words as they'll crop up again and again.

Stirrups

Stirrup irons help you to stay on, since both feet have an 'anchor'. They also make riding easier and more comfortable, particularly later on when you lift your seat out of the saddle for the rising trot or for jumping. The length of stirrup you adopt is partly down to what feels right for you, but there are general guidelines.

Testing the length

To test the stirrup length before you mount, stand facing the saddle on the right side of the pony. With your right hand make a fist and rest your knuckles on the stirrup bar (where the stirrup leathers are attached to the saddle).

Lift the stirrup leather and hold it against the length of your right arm.

The iron should reach to your armpit, if it doesn't, adjust the length of the leather, then repeat on the left side.

In the saddle

Since you may need to lengthen the stirrups to mount, you can also test the length once you're in the saddle. Take your foot out of the stirrup iron and let it hang down naturally. Both leathers should be the same length, with the bottom of the iron level with your ankle. If they're uneven, too short or too long, undo the buckle, and move it up or down a notch or two.

Like adjusting the girth, you'll have to look down at the stirrup leather to start with. But practise until you can change the stirrup length by touch, with your foot in the iron and looking ahead.

Checking stirrup length

1 Put the knuckles of your right hand on the stirrup bar. Lift the stirrup leather and hold it against your arm – it should reach the armpit.

2 When mounted, remove your feet from the stirrup irons – the bottom of the iron should be level with your ankle bone.

MISTAKES!

Don't ride with stirrups that are too short. Short stirrups make you grip with your knees and rise out of the saddle.

Nor should your stirrups be too long, as you'll be thrown forward easily, and have a 'weak seat'.

THE CORRECT LENGTH

When the stirrups are the right length, they help you to position your legs securely and to keep your balance.

Holding the reins

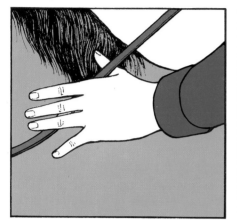

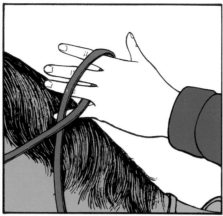

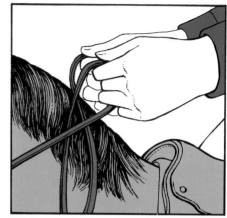

1 Place the rein in the palm of your hand and tuck your thumb and little finger underneath.

2 Loop the loose rein over your index finger. Your thumb and little finger should be outside the rein.

3 Hold your hands sideways, with thumbs on top as if you were holding the handles of two mugs.

MISTAKES!

Don't hold the reins upside down. You won't have proper control.

Don't let your hands drop, and keep your elbows close against your sides.

Never ride with your hands flat – this gives you little feel or control.

Your hands

Depending on how much progress you have made, the instructor might ask you to take up a contact with the pony's mouth. Strictly speaking this should not be until you can maintain a balanced correct position – called an independent seat – without holding on.

Never use the pony's mouth, via the reins, to help you keep your balance. If you need to cling on, grasp the front of the saddle or the mane. It is better to take longer and do it properly than to rush on before you've mastered the basics.

Holding the reins

To take up a contact you have to shorten the reins until you can feel a little weight on the end. Run the reins through each hand so that your middle three fingers close around them, with thumbs and little fingers outside.

Your hands should be about 10cm (4in) above the withers (the bony ridge in front of the saddle at the base of the mane). Hold the reins a few centimetres apart, one either side of the pony's neck. Keep your elbows relaxed and close to your sides: there should be no daylight visible between them to someone standing behind you.

Your reins should feel like pieces of elastic. As the horse nods his head in rhythm with the walk, your hand should give and take; the 'elastic' stretches and returns but it never pulls and never goes slack. You should attempt to maintain a constant feel on the reins, even at a halt.

The contact you have with the horse's mouth is there to contain the energy which you create in the horse's 'engine' – the hindquarters. The energy comes forward through the horse and it is your hands via the reins and bit that control it. To understand fully the marvellous sensation of controlling a horse takes a lifetime. That's what makes it all so fascinating!

 **IMAGINARY LINE**

When you're holding the reins correctly, you can trace a straight line from the elbows, down your arms, along the reins to the bit. If possible, ask someone to take a photograph of you so you can check your position.

21

Stopping and dismounting

An essential part of learning to ride is knowing how to ask your pony to stop. You should also know how to dismount safely.

'Talking' to your pony

Your hands control the pony's forehand (the front of the body) and slow him down, and your legs control his hindquarters and speed him up.

Your hands send messages to the pony through his mouth. They tell him to change direction, and they also slacken his pace. Your reins are like telegraph wires and should only be used to communicate – never to keep your balance.

Balancing

In other sports such as dancing and gymnastics you use your hands and arms to balance the rest of your body. In riding this is not possible. If your hands and arms move to help you keep your balance it will certainly be confusing and possibly painful for your pony. Also, if you hang on to the reins to keep your balance, it hurts the pony's mouth.

Preparing to stop

Always remember that asking your pony to stop is not just a matter of pulling on the reins. Before the pony stops you have to prepare and co-ordinate the natural aids – your hands and legs. And to do that you need a secure and well-balanced seat.

▼ **As you dismount,** remember to bend your knees to soften the impact when you land, and to keep hold of the reins!

As your pony walks along, make sure that you are sitting correctly before giving the aids to halt. Sit down into the deepest part of the saddle, and remember to keep your back straight. Sitting alert and upright brings the pony to attention, and lets him know that further instructions are coming.

Check that you have a contact with the pony's mouth. This means that you are able to feel his head movements without restricting them. If your elbows stick out behind your body before you feel any contact, your reins are too long. And if you're having to lean forward, your reins are too short.

Coming to a halt

Once you are happy that your position is correct at the walk, and you are ready to halt, relax your buttocks so they feel heavier in the saddle. Close both legs against the pony's sides and gently apply pressure on the reins. Saying 'whoa' in a soothing voice also helps.

Don't tug

Don't just tug on the reins. Resist with your hands by easing gently on and off the reins until the pony stops. Imagine that your hands are squeezing a sponge. If you pull in a jerky way, the pony is more likely to lean on your hand and pull against you. Be careful, too, not to pull back. The pony is stronger than the rider and will just resist if you try to force him to obey.

The moment you feel the pony stop, relax your hands and allow him to stand still for a short while. If you don't relax your hands you may confuse the pony into reversing. Your legs resting (not squeezing) against his sides help to say 'not backward'. Don't be cross with the pony if he doesn't understand your signals – it's probably your fault!

Getting off the pony

There is a proper way to get off a pony. It's the safest way to dismount and is the most comfortable for both you and the pony.

It is usual to dismount from the near (left) side of your pony, but practise dismounting from both sides. This also stands you in good stead when speed is important in, say, a relay competition at a gymkhana or in an emergency.

To dismount from the off (right) side the normal procedure is reversed. You must still halt and take both feet out of the stirrups. Put your reins into your right hand, place your left hand on the pommel and swing your left leg behind you.

MISTAKES!

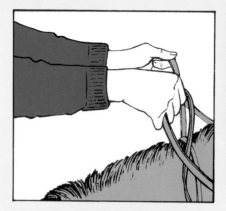

Don't flap your arms about when asking the pony to stop. A horse's mouth is delicate and rough treatment makes him insensitive to your instructions.

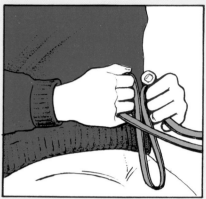

Don't have your reins too long as you won't have a proper contact. If you can't feel the pony's mouth, your hands won't be effective as aids.

Dismounting

1 First make sure that you have given the aids to halt and that your pony is standing perfectly still. Take both feet from the stirrup irons.

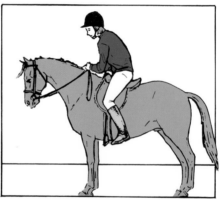

2 To dismount from the near (left) side of your pony, put both reins into your left hand so that you maintain complete control all the time. Place your right hand on the pommel (front of the saddle).

MISTAKES!

Never dismount by swinging your leg over the front of the saddle. It may look adventurous and easier, but remember that you have no control over the pony at all.

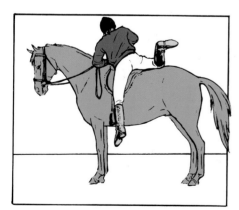

3 Swing your right leg behind you, over the saddle and the pony's back, and spring lightly to the ground. Remember to lift your leg high enough to avoid kicking the pony as you dismount.

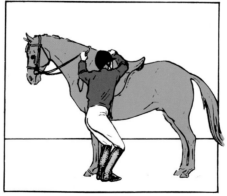

4 When jumping to the ground bend your knees so that you land lightly and don't jar your legs. Remember to keep control of your pony by holding the reins in your left hand.

Don't forget to take your left foot out of the stirrup. If the pony moves off with your foot lodged in the stirrup iron, you can be dragged with him.

Handling the pony

Part of the fun of riding is learning how to handle a pony. There are general rules that you should follow on what to do for safety and efficiency.

Treat all ponies with respect, but be particularly careful with ones you don't know. It's the unexpected that worries them so, whenever you're near a pony, let him know you are there. Try to approach him at the shoulder so he can see you clearly, speak to him and pat and reassure him.

It's best to stand close to the pony; if you stand a few feet away and he kicks, you receive the full force! If you need to get down low, crouch rather than kneel.

➤ **Leading the pony:**
When leading in a bridle, pass the reins over the pony's head and hold them with your right hand a short distance from the bit. Take the spare end of the rein (or rope, if the pony is in a headcollar) in your left hand. Don't pull, but walk by his shoulder and say 'walk on' in a firm, encouraging tone.

➤ **Giving a titbit:**
Always feed titbits from the flat of your palm — even a gentle, friendly pony can mistake a curled-up finger for part of the snack.

▼ **Where to stand:**
Try not to stand directly behind a horse — stand sideways on and place a hand on his hindquarters so he knows you're there.

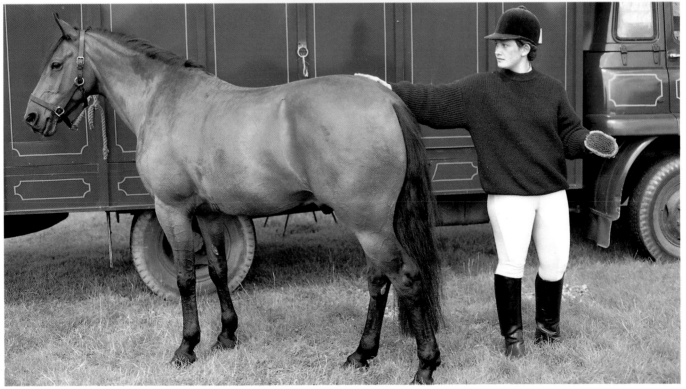

How to make turns

Beginners start by learning to sit quietly, whether the pony is walking or standing, keeping their backs straight and their heads up, their hands and legs still. The next stage is to ask the pony to turn either from a halt or at a walk.

Off the lunge

To practise turns, your pony will probably come off the lunge rein. This means you are in control of the pony – although your instructor should be on hand to help if you get in a muddle. Allow yourself 'thinking' time; don't rush into anything, and you'll be fine.

Natural aids

To ask your pony to turn, use your legs, hands and seat. These are called the 'natural aids'.

Your legs make the pony go forward. If you squeeze on the pony's sides with the lower part of your leg, he should move off in a straight line. Squeeze with your legs, relax, then squeeze again, until the pony responds. Then let your legs rest close to his sides. Remember to keep your toes pointing forward.

If the pony doesn't walk on when you ask, it may be that you are accidentally pulling on the reins at the same time as squeezing with your legs. If you are tense, it is all too easy to give the pony confused signals. This is why you should think before you act and tell yourself to relax first.

Check you are holding the reins correctly – your hands held sideways so that your thumbs are uppermost, and the reins running through each hand with your middle three fingers closed round them. They should be just tight enough to feel the pony's mouth and head movements without restricting him. Make sure your hands are in the right place, about 10cm (4in) above the withers, and the same distance apart.

Sit down when you use your legs and hands. In this way, your seat encourages the pony to go forward. All you need to do at this stage is sit firmly in the saddle and not perch as though you were on a drawing pin!

Your voice

The voice is also a natural aid: talking to the pony is quite acceptable, and your instructor may do this a lot at first. The voice, however, doesn't make a pony

▼ Turning in an arena: Having a lesson in an enclosed space means you can practise turns continually – either by moving in a circle, or by making sharper changes of direction in a square or rectangle.

Giving signals

The hands, legs, seat and voice are known as natural aids because they 'aid' the pony's understanding of what you want him to do. The term describes both the way you give signals to the pony and the signals themselves.

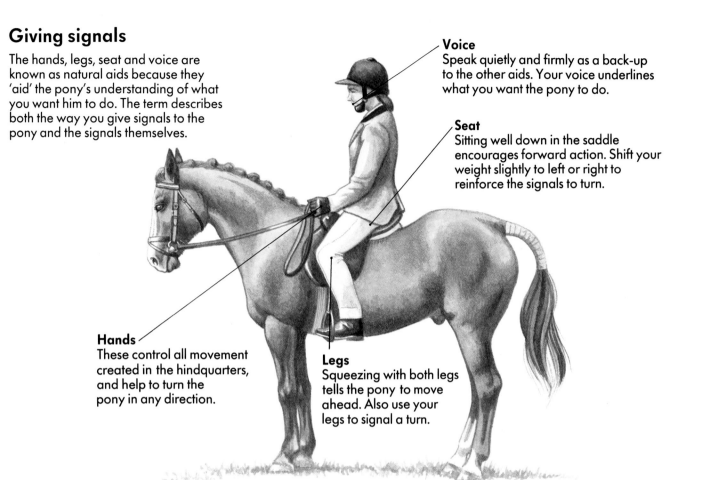

Voice
Speak quietly and firmly as a back-up to the other aids. Your voice underlines what you want the pony to do.

Seat
Sitting well down in the saddle encourages forward action. Shift your weight slightly to left or right to reinforce the signals to turn.

Hands
These control all movement created in the hindquarters, and help to turn the pony in any direction.

Legs
Squeezing with both legs tells the pony to move ahead. Also use your legs to signal a turn.

★ REIN MARKERS
When you're concentrating on lots of new things at once, it helps to know your reins are the right length.

Once your instructor has made sure that your hands are where they should be, mark the correct points with a couple of elastic bands or some string. Then, no matter what happens, you can always see where your hands should be!

The aids for turning

▲ **Learning to combine all the aids** for turning requires a lot of practice. Think about what instruction you are going to give before you move and then give the aids clearly.

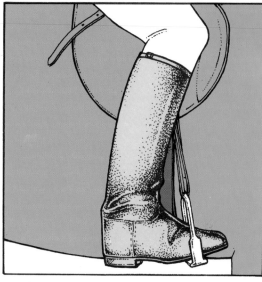

▲ **The inside leg** is the most important leg. It must be applied close to the girth. This leg keeps the horse moving forward and gives him something to bend around.

MISTAKES!

Don't lean to one side. This unbalances you and the pony.

Don't move your outside leg too far behind the girth.

move to the left or right which is why you use hands, legs, and seat.

How to turn

To turn left or right, you use a basic combination of one hand and one leg. For a left turn, use the left rein and left leg and for a right turn, the right rein and right leg.

The rein turns the pony's head to look where he is going. The leg (used by the girth as in a 'walk forward' signal) encourages him to keep moving and helps him to bend around your leg on the curve. The *outside* leg stops the horse's hindquarters moving out of line and propels him in the right direction.

Changing direction

When you tighten your hold slightly on one rein only, your pony turns his head without moving his feet. Gently try the other rein – the same thing happens.

Don't turn him too far or he has to move his feet to balance. Now straighten up and use both legs to move forward. As you come to a corner, turn your shoulders in line with the pony's. Keep your left leg by the girth and then 'feel' the left rein, as you did at a halt. You can turn corners!

Halfway round the turn stop telling the pony to go left. Look up and ride straight forward or you turn too much and go round in circles.

Shifting your weight is also a signal to turn. Very simply, if you sit to the left of the saddle, the pony wants to move to the left. Thinking about using hands and legs is enough at the moment. But, if you always remember to look through the pony's ears in the direction you want

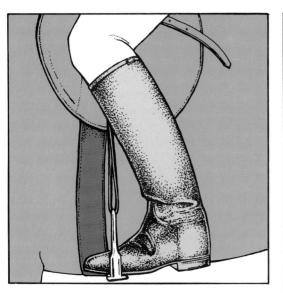

▲ **The outside leg** is placed just behind the girth. This stops the pony's hindquarters from swinging out, and encourages him round the turn.

Don't tug and lean back; a pony can't be forced to turn.

Don't hunch forward – it weakens your seat.

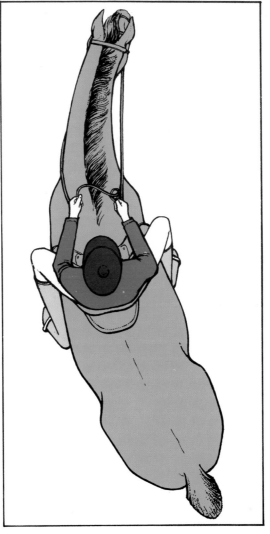

▲ **Your shoulders** should move with the pony in the direction you want to go. The inside hand turns the pony, while the outside hand restrains him and keeps the pace smooth.

 **ADAPT TO THE PONY**

No two ponies are alike. They all have minds of their own and may not *want* to do as they are told. Sometimes you need stronger legs or clearer rein aids.

The art of riding well is being able to adapt to these changes and to tune in to each new pony and his various moods. This is what makes ponies so much more rewarding than machines.

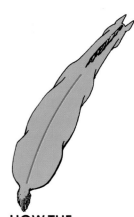

HOW THE PONY TURNS

When the pony bends correctly, his spine goes in the direction of the turn and he makes a smooth arc as he turns. If his head is jerked round to make him turn, this flowing movement cannot happen.

to go and turn your shoulders in that direction, you automatically start to use your weight correctly.

Supporting aids

Whether you are stopping or starting, turning left or turning right, you still have two arms and two legs which should be doing something all the time. Your 'spare' arm and leg are 'supporting' aids. They prevent the pony from over-reacting to your commands and they help to finish each change of direction or pace smoothly.

For instance, in a left turn, your outside hand keeps the rein from hanging in a loop and stops the pony turning too sharply. Your outside leg is placed further back than the inside one to stop the hindquarters swinging to the outside. Don't move your left leg back –

keep it forward near the girth. When you ask your pony to go forward, maintain a light feel on both reins to control the speed. This way, it is easy to make a series of smooth turns.

Good hands

One of the things that makes a rider look good is being able to ride without appearing to give instructions. This should be every rider's aim and comes mainly from having good hands.

Your hands are the link between you and the pony's mouth. If you hold the reins too stiffly or use them roughly, then at best it is hard for the pony to go smoothly and at worst you hurt him. Good hands are gentle and still so, from the start, try to make your signals a secret between you and your pony; other people don't need to see them.

The sitting and rising trot

With walking and turning mastered, it is time to move on to the trot. There are two ways of riding the pace: sitting or rising.

How the pony trots

The trot is a two-time pace, so all four legs advance in two movements. The pony springs from one diagonal pair of legs to the other and in between is a moment of suspension when he is completely off the ground. This is why trotting feels so much more bumpy than walking.

Sitting trot

To begin with, get the feel of the movement in sitting trot (a pony is often said to be 'in' a pace rather than 'at' it).

Your instructor will first make sure that you are sitting properly in the walk. To make the transition from walk to trot your reins should be slightly shorter than in the walk as the pony's head is a little higher in trot.

Close your legs against the pony's sides and he should begin to trot. If he doesn't, gently squeeze again, to underline what you want him to do. Firmly hold the front of the saddle (or the neck strap) with both hands, sit up tall and try to relax – especially your seat muscles. At first a few strides are enough. Then – when you know how bumpy the trot feels – have a rest!

Now trot for longer and count the beats to yourself. Bump, bump, bump, bump . . . one-two, one-two. Try counting out loud while you are trotting, but don't attempt to do anything more than sit still at this stage.

Your position

The basic position for sitting trot is exactly the same as in the walk or halt. Most people tighten up as the pony starts to trot – it's difficult not to as the pony is not only going faster but is moving around a lot more as well.

Keep your legs wrapped around the pony, so you don't get bounced off. Try not to grip with your knees, as this means your seat is more likely to be lifted out of the saddle. ➤

Holding the whip

The whip is an artificial aid, as opposed to the natural aids of your hands and legs. It is for backing up your leg aids when a pony fails to respond.

You should start with the whip in your inside hand (the left hand when you're circling left and vice versa). Hold the handle, and let the length of the whip rest against your thigh.

To pass the whip from one hand to another, put both reins into one hand (otherwise you might lose control of the pony) and exchange the whip. Then you can separate out the reins again.

Looking at the angle of the whip is a good way to check that your hands are in the correct position as you are riding. If the whip is dangling down the horse's shoulder, your hands are too upright. If it's sticking up, toward your hip, your hands are too flat and your elbows are probably sticking out!

You need quite a lot of riding practice before you use a whip. Once you do carry one, apply it as little possible and *never* use it to punish a horse.

▼ **The trot** is the bumpiest pace to begin with. Concentrate on sitting as still as possible, and remember to keep your back straight.

Rising trot

1 The rising trot is much more comfortable than the sitting trot, for both pony and rider, and a lot less tiring.

The idea behind rising is quite simple: stand as one pair of the pony's legs comes off the ground and sit as the same pair of legs returns to the ground. You can practise the rising trot in halt and walk. Stand up in your stirrups and *slowly* sit down again. Never use the reins to pull yourself up, as this will hurt the pony's mouth.

2 While you are learning to balance use a neck strap to keep you in position. You need this until you can stand and sit without collapsing on to the pony. A neck strap does not affect the pony and is better than clutching the mane because it puts your hands in much the same position as they are when holding the reins.

Stand up and sit down in beat with the pony's trot. As you did while you were sitting at the trot, count one-two, one-two until you get the rhythm. Your aim is to stand on one and sit on two.

3 As the pony makes the transition from walk to trot, you may lose your balance for a moment, especially during the first few lessons.

Keep working — say to yourself 'up-down, up-down' in time to the trot. Once you pick up the correct beat you'll notice that the pony pushes you out of the saddle just the right amount and it's quite effortless.

If sometimes you can and sometimes you can't rise to the trot, just keep on trying — practice soon makes perfect.

⭐ **INSTRUCTOR KNOW-HOW**
Riding school language can be confusing. You gain more from your early lessons if you understand what you're being asked to do! The arena (school) on the opposite page sets out some of the terms you'll hear. Never be afraid to ask if you are puzzled.
☐ You should also get to know the markers around the arena; the instructor will refer to them when directing the riders. An easy way to learn the letters can be found on page 135.
☐ Finally, do remember to thank the instructor at the end of your lesson.

The lower part of the leg makes the pony go faster or turn. If you grip with this part to stay on, the pony may speed up and you'll lose control.

The change from walk to trot may throw you back a little. You can correct this by pushing your stomach forward when you are ready to start trotting. Avoid *leaning* forward; this is a weak position and actually bounces you around more.

Transition to walk

Coming down to the walk is easier than the trot itself. Whether you have been rising or sitting you must always be in sitting trot for the transition to walk. Press down in your seat and resist a little on the reins — not too much or the pony stops! Close your legs against his sides to make sure that he keeps going forward.

You may be tipped forward as the pony slows down, so be ready. Sit back and relax. For the time being, keep hold of the neck strap or saddle until you are walking again.

Practising off the pony

You can practise the rising trot from the ground. Stand with your feet apart, toes forward, back straight, as though you were riding a tiny, invisible pony.

Start with your knees slightly bent. Now lower yourself toward the ground by bending your knees more, come up to your original position, go lower again and so on. This helps you to find your riding muscles.

What can go wrong?

When you're trying to rise to the trot, don't lift your seat too high out of the saddle. Stay as close as you can, without losing your 'rise'.

Another fault is working too hard with your shoulders so your upper body is wagging backward and forward as you sit and rise.

Try to push your weight down into your heels so that you use your leg muscles and not your arms to pull yourself up. Imagine you have something balanced on your head — a book or a bucket of icy cold water.

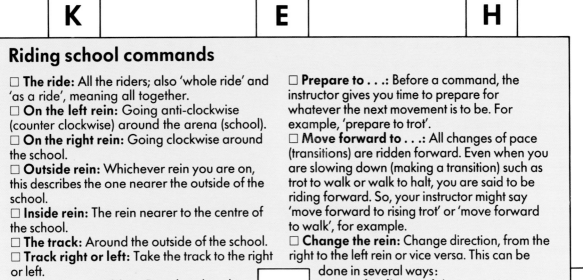

K   **E**   **H**

Riding school commands

☐ **The ride:** All the riders; also 'whole ride' and 'as a ride', meaning all together.

☐ **On the left rein:** Going anti-clockwise (counter clockwise) around the arena (school).

☐ **On the right rein:** Going clockwise around the school.

☐ **Outside rein:** Whichever rein you are on, this describes the one nearer the outside of the school.

☐ **Inside rein:** The rein nearer to the centre of the school.

☐ **The track:** Around the outside of the school.

☐ **Track right or left:** Take the track to the right or left.

☐ **Prove your position:** Put a hand on the pommel and pull yourself down so you are sitting deeply in the saddle.

☐ **Shorten the reins:** Make the length of rein between your hand and the bit short enough to give you better contact with the horse's mouth.

☐ **Keep your distance** or **Watch your distances:** Leave about one horse's length between you and the rider in front.

☐ **Leading file:** The rider in front.

☐ **Leading files in succession:** One after another.

☐ **To the rear of the ride:** Ride alone around the school and join the others at the back.

☐ **Prepare to . . .:** Before a command, the instructor gives you time to prepare for whatever the next movement is to be. For example, 'prepare to trot'.

☐ **Move forward to . . .:** All changes of pace (transitions) are ridden forward. Even when you are slowing down (making a transition) such as trot to walk or walk to halt, you are said to be riding forward. So, your instructor might say 'move forward to rising trot' or 'move forward to walk', for example.

☐ **Change the rein:** Change direction, from the right to the left rein or vice versa. This can be done in several ways:

   across the diagonal: between K-M or F-H, passing through X.

   across the centre of the school: E-X-B or B-X-E.

down the centre of the line: A-X-C or C-X-A.

☐ **20-metre circle:** This usually means a circle covering half a 20×40-metre school, touching the track at C or A and passing through X.

☐ **Circle in the centre of the school:** A circle starting at E or B with X as the centre.

☐ **Three-loop serpentine:** A double S which starts at A or C.

☐ **Turn in and halt:** Turn off the track at right angles and halt.

A   **X**   **C**

F   **B**   **M**

Diagonals

Rising to the trot means that you stand and sit as the same diagonal pair of legs comes off the ground and goes back to the ground.

The girl pictured above is riding on the *right* diagonal. This means that she sits while the *off* (right) fore and *near* (left) hind are on the ground (marked in red in the first and third pictures). She stands when the near fore and off hind (marked in red in the centre picture) are on the ground.

You should change diagonals every so often so your muscles and your pony's build up evenly. To swap the diagonal, sit for an extra beat. Count it to yourself, up-down, up-down, up-*down-down*, up-down.

Balancing is easier for the pony if you sit on the *outside* diagonal (right diagonal on a left circle, left diagonal on a right circle). So change the diagonal every time you change rein (direction).

Until you can feel how the pony's legs are moving, have a look at his shoulders as he walks and trots. When a foreleg is on the ground, that shoulder moves toward the saddle. As the foot is lifted, the shoulder swings away.

In rising trot, sit as the outside shoulder comes back toward you, stand as it swings away.

Get into the habit of always checking your diagonal as soon as you start rising to the trot.

From trot to canter

**! WHERE TO
• CANTER**

No matter how much you enjoy cantering, remember the horse's well-being.

The canter should only be attempted on suitable ground, otherwise the pony's legs will be jarred. Soft ground is best, and you must never canter on a road surface.

**WATCHING
OTHER PONIES**

It always helps to watch other people riding in canter and to notice how the pony's legs move. Just watch the two front legs to begin with. It is quite easy to see the inside foreleg going ahead of the outside foreleg.

Ponies loose in a paddock naturally canter on the correct leg, changing lead whenever they change direction. If they don't change lead, they generally break into a trot for a few strides when making a turn.

Once you are used to the rhythm, cantering is more comfortable than trotting. Not many people can run fast enough to lead you for your first canter, which also makes it much more exciting than the first trot!

The change of pace

By now you are used to the difference in feel between the walk and the trot. There is just as big a change in feel from trot to canter. Because the canter is faster, everything happens more quickly. So you need to be that bit better balanced and more confident than for the slower paces.

The walk gives you a gentle rolling feel from side to side as well as forward; the trot is a faster and bouncier gait. The canter is less bouncy but more rocking. With each step the pony takes you feel a stronger push from the hindlegs. This rocks your body backward and forward slightly but in rhythm.

The aids for canter

To prepare for canter, ride your pony forward in rising trot, making full use of all four corners of the arena. Change to sitting trot, and steady just a little.

Sitting to the trot lets your pony know that a change is coming. Rising trot emphasizes the two-time rhythm, making it harder for him to change into the three-time action of canter. And from your point of view, it is easier to remain seated in canter if you are already

sitting firmly in the saddle for the trot.

As you come to the second corner of the short side of the arena, give the aids for canter. Sit back and put your inside leg in the forward position (on the girth). Return your outside leg to behind the girth.

As the pony breaks into canter, keep sitting back. Push your heels down and try not to tighten up too much. Let yourself rock gently in rhythm with the movement. One long straight side of the arena is enough for the first canter. At this stage, too, it is better to hold the saddle or neck strap with one hand while you get used to the new movement.

Position in the saddle

The position in the saddle for canter is the same as for sitting trot. So, before

▲ **Cantering in an arena** when you are learning means you don't have to worry about the pony rushing off with you as you learn this new and exciting pace.

How to sit

The position you should be in for canter is much the same as for the sitting trot. However, because the canter is a faster movement, you have to be more careful about getting your position right. Any mistakes are accentuated.

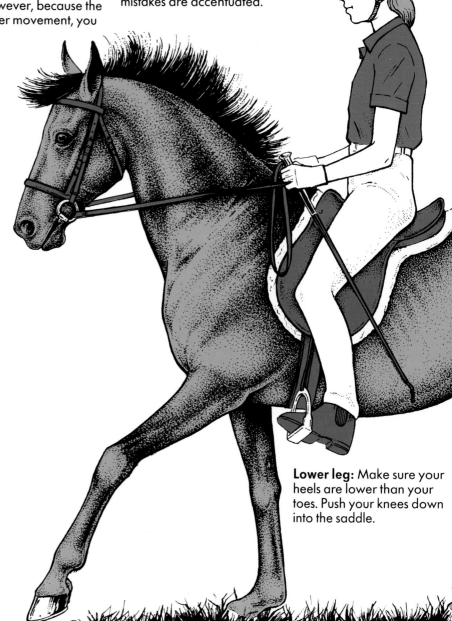

Lower leg: Make sure your heels are lower than your toes. Push your knees down into the saddle.

MISTAKES!

Don't lean back, with your legs forward in an effort to relax. This weak position gives no control.

Bumping around in the saddle, because of an insecure seat, unbalances the pony too.

cantering, think about any weaknesses you have in your position for trot. These are shown up to an even greater extent in canter.

If you tend to lean *forward* and move your legs too far back, you'll be bounced forward even more in canter. If you tend to lean *back* and push your legs forward, then you will find yourself hanging on hard to the saddle.

Keep the best position you can, but don't tense your muscles. Sit up straight, push your knees down the saddle and your heels down lower than your toes. Always remember to look up and in the direction you are going.

When you've managed your first canter in a straight line, try cantering right round the arena. Just push a little more weight into your inside knee and heel as you come to the corners so that the pony keeps going.

The transition to trot

To make the transition to trot, relax your legs into the normal position on the pony's sides, and use the outside rein to slow down. The transition from canter to trot feels more bumpy than trot to canter. You can make it much smoother

Look ahead and only glance down briefly when you have to check the leading leg.

Your seat: Sit back, but don't tighten up too much – try to relax your seat and lower back muscles without losing your position. You must remain firmly in the saddle. Rock gently with the rhythm of the canter. All the movement should come from the small of your back.

Left and right canter

Canter left means the pony leads with his left foreleg. The full sequence is then off hind, right diagonal (off fore and near hind together) and lastly the near fore. This is followed by a moment of suspension in which all four legs are off the ground at once.

Canter right is exactly the opposite, with the right foreleg leading. Although the leading leg is the last leg down in the sequence, it is called the leading leg because it appears to be out in front.

Practise changing from one leg to the other. Go into sitting trot, put your right leg on the girth and your left leg behind. Then repeat this exercise, reversing your leg aids. It helps to have the pony looking in the direction of the turn. Your outside rein is steadying the pony, so open and close the fingers of your inside hand to ask for the bend.

▼ Cantering on the wrong leg can make the pony stumble on a turn.

ONE-SIDED PONIES

If a pony is stiff or simply strong-willed, he may only want to canter on one leg. He is what is called a 'one-sided' pony, and tells you which leg he wants to lead on, rather than you telling him!

Once you have made sure that your aids are correct, make him go round a bend *toward* the leg you want to lead on. This way, his favourite leg is on the outside. Be firm with your outside leg to prevent him swinging outward and away from your instructions. Keep riding in a large circle until he does as you ask.

by riding into rising trot first to stop you jolting around in the saddle.

How the canter works

Using your inside leg on the girth keeps the pony active and working toward the outside of the arena. The outside leg, in moving back, asks the pony to strike off on the correct leading leg.

Remember the sequence of footfalls for the canter. The horse's outside hind-leg strikes off first. It is followed by the outside diagonal pair of legs and lastly, the inside foreleg. This is known as the leading leg.

It is important for the pony's balance that the inside fore is the leading leg. If the pony is made to canter on the wrong leg in a turn he may lose his balance and stumble. Asking for canter on a corner helps him to lead correctly, even if your aids are unclear to start with.

You can spot the leading leg while you are in canter. From the saddle, glance down at the pony's shoulders. Check whether the inside shoulder is slightly in advance of the outside shoulder. If it is, you can safely ride round on a corner. But if the outside shoulder appears to be forward, return to trot and start again.

Galloping – top speed

▲ **Being able to gallop** is a good confidence booster as well as being great fun!

Learning to gallop is what most new riders dream about. It's a very exciting stage to reach – fast and fun and relatively easy.

How the gallop feels

The gallop feels quite steady because the pony's back hardly moves. Instead, he stretches forward with his head and neck to allow for the longer strides and greater reach of the front legs. If the trot is an up-and-down movement, and the canter a rocking action, then the gallop feels horizontal.

Before you gallop

Before attempting to gallop, you should be sure of yourself in canter. You must feel confident – able to sit reasonably still without holding on and capable of riding turns and transitions in and out of canter.

If your balance is a bit shaky when the pony canters faster or makes a turn unexpectedly, then you aren't ready! However impatient you are to tackle the gallop, wait until you are in control while cantering before increasing the speed.

When you are learning to gallop, you must wear a skull cap – this item is an essential safety precaution once you begin to ride the faster paces.

Another point to remember before you start is that galloping is demanding for the pony. It puts a strain on his muscles, limbs, heart and lungs. He must be fit enough to move at speed and, even then, galloping should be limited.

The gallop

The gallop is a variation of the canter rather than a separate pace. The differences are that the pony's legs move one at a time – so it is a four-time movement – and obviously it's faster too!

There are two possible patterns for the legs to move in, depending on which hindleg strikes off: one hindleg (**1**), the other hindleg (**2**), the foreleg diagonal to this (**3**) and finally the other foreleg (**4**).

Position in the saddle

For the gallop you need to ride in a 'forward' position. So reach down and shorten your stirrups one or two holes, lean forward and take your weight out of the saddle.

It helps to grip slightly with your knees and push down on to your heels and big toe joint rather than the outside edge of your foot. With your heels down, press your knees into the knee rolls (the pads at the front of the saddle flaps which are designed to give the rider extra security).

Keep your back straight and look ahead. Your hands should be further forward and up on the pony's neck. This prevents you from shooting straight over the top and on to the ground if the pony stops suddenly. Grasp a handful of mane if you want.

Check your position

Try this position first in halt until you feel comfortable and balanced, then in walk, trot and finally canter. It is quite a tiring posture for your leg muscles but should not affect you otherwise. If your back aches, think about your position as it probably needs altering.

Transition to gallop

So far, you have learnt to sit with a straight line running down through your shoulder, hip and heel.

In gallop you have to think about another straight line, one that goes through your shoulder, knee and ankle. Ride into gallop from a balanced canter. All you need to do is push on, squeezing with both legs.

Gradually increase the speed, allowing your hands to go forward as the length of stride increases. You hardly

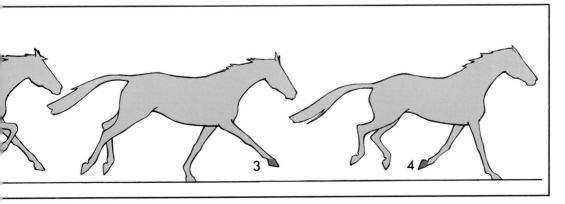

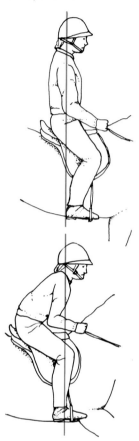

► **The position for gallop** is different from anything you've learnt so far, and you must shorten your stirrups for it.

NEW LINE
Being in gallop means there is a new straight line to aim for. Instead of the line going through your shoulder, hip and heel, the position for gallop should produce a line which travels through your shoulder, knee and ankle.

Once you have shortened the stirrups, ask your instructor to check that you have this line. The line may slope but should not approach the horizontal or you will fall off!

notice the transition. Galloping feels very smooth as the gait becomes more level and powerful. You can feel the pony's neck muscles harden as he uses more energy.

Slowing down

Just like the canter, slowing down is a little more difficult than speeding up, simply because you are going so fast and you don't have so much time.

A lively pony who is enjoying the gallop might try to ignore your instructions at first, but if you give the aids for stopping correctly, he has to slow down! A pony needs a fairly straight line to keep galloping, so if you need to you can make him slow down by bringing him gradually into a turn.

Making the transition

Check the speed with your outside rein. Begin to sit back by moving your seat closer to the saddle and putting your shoulders up. Always keep as much weight as possible in your knees and heels and keep your knees tucked into the knee rolls. On the turn, place more weight on your inside leg than the

40

outside leg. Remember to look up!

Without jerking, check and ease, gradually slowing down all the time. You need to allow plenty of room to stop so that the transition is smooth. Don't pull hard on both reins together without frequently easing the contact. If you just haul steadily, the pony could lean on your hands and carry on galloping.

You may have to turn the pony to slow down. Simply make your circle smaller and smaller until you are back in canter and then in trot. If you feel him bunch up, ready to go again, turn his head and he won't be able to gallop.

If you do feel unsafe, shorten the inside rein and brace your hand against the pony's neck. This leaves your outside hand free to check the pony. It also means that if he stops abruptly you cannot fall forward.

Once you have settled him down again, try to ride with a light contact. A pull on the reins creates a 'tug of war' which is tiring and usually won by the superior strength of the pony.

▼ **Turning the pony** is an effective way of stopping him, because he needs a straight line to keep galloping.

Where to gallop

You can learn to gallop in a large arena, but if you go further afield, take care to find a site that is suitable.

☐ Never gallop anywhere near traffic.

☐ Check the area carefully first by riding around in walk, to make sure the ground is not too hard.

☐ Look out for anything that could cause stumbling — ruts, potholes, boggy areas or large stones.

☐ Avoid galloping downhill — level ground or gently rising ground is best.

☐ Never gallop toward a ditch or fence that is not clearly visible from a distance.

☐ Make sure you have room to turn.

☐ Ride with at least one experienced person. Set off together, with the more experienced rider just ahead of you. Ponies galloping side by side tend to race so that stopping can be quite difficult. If one is slightly in front, when the first pony slows down, the other wants to slacken the pace too. This means you stay in full control.

☐ Vary the places where you gallop and don't gallop too often. Frequently riding at full speed makes your pony 'hot up' (fuss and pull at the bit).

☐ It must always be your decision, and not the pony's, as to whether you gallop or not. It is a good idea to walk the route after you have galloped it. This gives the pony a chance to cool down and relax, as well as teaching him good habits.

▼ Give your pony a thank-you hug after a good gallop!

DIFFERENT STYLES
There are three basic ways of riding a gallop which you may have already spotted.

🐴 The first style is the one described in this chapter, and is the easiest to learn and the most practical. It is used by eventers when riding cross country. This position is comfortable for horse and rider and the rider is in control. It is also a safe position for jumping.

★ The second style is used in the show ring. The rider remains sitting up very straight, to make the horse look strong and big-striding. It is a specialist style, only suitable for experienced riders and over short distances.

★ The most extreme is that of a jockey who rides with very short stirrups. This is much harder than it looks. The idea is to cut down wind resistance and put the least strain on the horse. Again, this is for specialist riding only, not for the everyday rider.

Exercises in the saddle

Having mastered the basics of riding, it is a good idea to do some simple exercises to improve your balance and control.

Why exercise?

At first, you probably ache after a lesson because your muscles are doing work they never had to do before. These exercises will help make you stronger and more supple so riding becomes easier and more natural.

Also, these exercises help you to develop a good seat, by building up suppleness, balance and poise (sitting up straight).

Before you start

You should remember to warm up before exercising for any sport. Riding is no exception. If you sit still for too long without moving, your muscles stiffen up. Ride for a few minutes before you start your exercises.

All these movements should be done slowly to avoid strain. Increase the number of times you do each one as you get fitter. Feel as though you have worked and stretched but do not hurt yourself.

If you are nervous about trying a new exercise, ask your teacher to help. Don't give up too easily: it's amazing how much your confidence improves if you are prepared to have a go.

For all the exercises in this chapter, you have to let go of the reins. Tie them in a knot out of the way and make sure someone holds the pony so he does not move off suddenly.

EXERCISES ON THE LUNGE

If you are lucky enough to be having lunge lessons, then you can practise *Touching Poll and Tail* on the lunge in walk.

You may find the exercise harder than it looks. Try it in halt first with someone holding the pony's head. Even when you are quite accomplished, don't attempt *Half Scissors, Lying Backward and Forward* or *Round the World* in anything but halt or you'll find yourself on the ground!

► **Crossing the stirrups:** For exercises where stirrups aren't used, cross the irons in front of the saddle so you don't get bruised ankles. Flapping stirrups may also upset the pony.

When the exercise is over, uncross the stirrups and try to put your feet back into them without looking down or turning the stirrup with your hand. This is a useful trick to perfect.

Half Scissors

This exercise, called *Half Scissors* because of the way your legs move, is an effective way of improving your co-ordination and suppleness. It is very important that somebody holds the pony for you throughout the exercise as you have no control over him.

1 Before starting the exercise, cross the stirrups. Hold on to the pommel with your left hand. Hold on behind with your right hand to maintain your balance. Swing your right leg over the front of the saddle.

2 Bring your right leg all the way over to the left, without kicking the pony's neck, so both legs are on the same side. When you need to, adjust the position of your hands to keep your body balanced.

3 When both legs are on the same side, turn your body round so that you are facing the saddle. Keep your legs straight and suspended in the air — at no point must your feet touch the ground.

Your arms carry all the weight during this exercise.

4 At this stage it's as if you are halfway through mounting, but without stirrups. Swing your right leg up and over the pony's hindquarters. Then you are back in your original position.

5 Now you are ready to do the exercise the other way round. Simply start with your left leg rather than the right — but don't do this exercise too many times to begin with, as it's quite a strain!

Round the World

This is another good exercise for building up suppleness and making you feel at home in the saddle.

Throughout the exercise, try to keep one hand on the pommel and one hand on the cantle to steady yourself.

1 Cross the stirrups and move your right leg over the pony's neck. Swing yourself sideways, until both legs are together and your back is against the pony's near side.

2 Carefully lift your left leg over the pony's hindquarters. You will soon see why this series of movements is called *Round the World*!

3 At this stage you should be sitting as though you had mounted the pony the wrong way, facing the tail. Try hard to keep your back straight while moving around and changing position on the saddle.

4 Next, swing your right leg up and over the back of the pony. As you become more and more tired toward the end of this exercise, take extra care not to bump or kick him.

5 You are now sitting sideways again, but facing in the opposite direction, with both legs on the pony's off side. Remember to keep your head up and don't round your shoulders.

6 Finally, lift your left leg over the pony's neck and you're back where you started. At first you'll feel slow and clumsy doing this exercise, but the more you practise the easier it will become!

Lying Backward and Forward

1 Attempt this exercise only when you feel confident about the previous ones. You can't hold on in this exercise so you need to be well balanced.

Start by sitting deep in the saddle, with your arms by your sides. Carefully lean backward until you are lying along the pony's back.

Then sit up in the saddle, *without* using your arms or legs to help you.

2 Now lean forward along the neck of the pony. Try to keep your knees and feet in position. If you feel able to, cross your arms behind your back and push yourself back into a sitting position, unaided by your arms.

Lying backward and forward without using your arms or your legs to help you back into sitting position strengthens your stomach muscles better than any other exercise. It's a real effort at first, but it's worth it!

Touching Poll and Tail

1 You *must* have your feet in the stirrups for this exercise so uncross them before you do anything else. You might want to hold on with your free hand to start with.

Stretch up with one hand above your head. Keeping your back straight and your lower leg still, stretch forward and down to place your hand between the pony's ears, on the poll. If you can't reach, push your hand along the pony's mane as far as you can. Hold for a few seconds, then sit up.

2 Raise your hand above your head again. Stretch over and round behind you, watching your hand, to touch the top of the pony's tail. Once again, raise your hand above your head and then let your arm drop to your side. Repeat with the other hand.

This will strengthen your back and legs and improve your balance. Remember to push your heels down throughout and keep your legs in position.

Your first jumping lesson

► **Eddie Macken and Carrolls Flight**, soaring over the type of complex jump only found at top competitive levels.

HOW A HORSE JUMPS

The best way to describe how a horse jumps is to imagine a big stride of canter. Cantering is a series of small leaps forward. A bigger leap is all that is necessary to clear an obstacle. So if you can already ride well in canter you are more than halfway to jumping over a small fence.

Jumping is an important part of learning to ride. Knowing how to jump makes you feel more confident, it helps when you ride outside the school – and find small branches or ditches across your path – and it's almost always exciting.

How to sit

You need to learn the jumping position to help your pony keep his balance and to stay secure in the saddle. It is the same basic position as for galloping. Instead of sitting up straight, just lean forward, letting your heels and knees take your weight.

It is much easier to sit correctly if your stirrups are shorter. One or two holes are enough at first. Shorten your reins too, so that your hands are further forward up the pony's neck. It's important to feel comfortable in this position, so start by practising while your pony is standing still.

For your first proper jump it's a good idea to hold on to the pony's mane, or a neck strap, until you get used to the feel of the movement. This gives you an idea of where your hands should be as well – not *too* far forward or you lose your balance when you let go! Remember to keep your back flat, not rounded, and look up and forward.

Your first practice session

1 When you are positioning poles on the ground, put them about 1m (1yd) apart, depending on the size of the pony.

2 Make sure you give your pony a good look at the poles so he knows what's in store for him. Secure each pole by placing a few small stones underneath to stop it rolling if he misses his footing.

3 Lead the pony over the poles. He'll soon learn what he's meant to do and will pick up his feet to avoid the poles.

4 Aim for the middle of the poles and walk straight over them. Look up and ahead. Do this exercise until you feel confident and the pony picks his feet up over every pole — but don't let him get bored.

The stages of a jump

A jump can be split into five phases. If you see exactly how a horse jumps you'll understand how important it is not to upset his balance or impede his movements.

approach   take off   time in the a

□ The **approach** — the pony lowers his head to judge the position and height of the jump.
□ Next comes the **take off**, when the front feet leave the ground and the horse raises his head. This occurs roughly the same distance from a jump as its height – for example, 60cm (2ft) away for a jump 60cm (2ft) high.
□ During **time in the air** the pony tucks up his feet, lowers his head, stretches his neck and rounds his back.
□ Then comes the **landing**, one front foot at a time, with the pony's head coming up again.
□ Finally, there is the **follow through** as the pony takes his first stride away from the fence. This final stage becomes important when jumping a series of fences.

Poles on the ground

Although you will probably be given an experienced jumping pony to begin with, ponies have to be taught to jump too, so take care to be patient and kind.

When you place a pole on the ground, prevent it from rolling about by wedging something underneath it – a few pebbles or tufts of grass. If your pony accidentally kicks or treads on a pole that isn't secured, he could fall over as it rolls under his feet.

Start with one pole on the ground. Take the pony to the pole and let him look at it first. Then lead him over it. If you begin in this way, you will find out how much the pony already knows and how he is likely to behave when you ask him to jump.

Practise riding a good approach to a jump. In walk, aim straight for the middle of a single pole and ride straight on afterwards. When you can manage all this with one pole, place several out in a line, at about 1m (1yd) apart – less if your pony is small. Now try walking over them.

After this, try putting several poles around the arena or field to practise riding turns and coming in straight. Get used to going into jumping position as you come up to and over each pole.

Attempt only one or two of these new exercises at the first lesson. Restrict the time you spend jumping to about 15 minutes, otherwise the pony may become tired and bored.

As you practise, vary the position of your poles and stop repeating an exercise once you have got it right. If your pony gets fed up he may start misbehaving by kicking the poles around or refusing – stopping or running past.

The aids for jumping

The aids for jumping are surprisingly simple. Think about them from the start, even though you are still working on the flat. You should use both legs together on the approach, pushing on a little for the last few strides. Always remember to look up and allow your pony to stretch his neck.

Consider the following points while you are walking over poles on the ground. By getting into good habits at this early stage, the correct jumping technique will come naturally when you tackle higher obstacles at a faster pace.
● Make sure you ride straight – don't come in at an angle.
● Use your legs in rhythm with the pony and avoid flapping and kicking when your pony is trying to concentrate.
● Be careful not to hang on to the reins. This hurts the pony as it pulls his head up, hollows his back and makes him drop his hindlegs down on the jump.
● After a jump (the follow through), look ahead and keep going! It sounds obvious, but many riders fail to get a clear round at the very last jump because they forget to ride on.
● Remember that good jumping is always the result of careful preparation. A well-schooled pony, confidently and properly ridden, finds jumping easy and enjoyable.

landing

follow through

The jumping position

This is the best position to be in while jumping — the pony remains balanced, and you stay securely in the saddle.

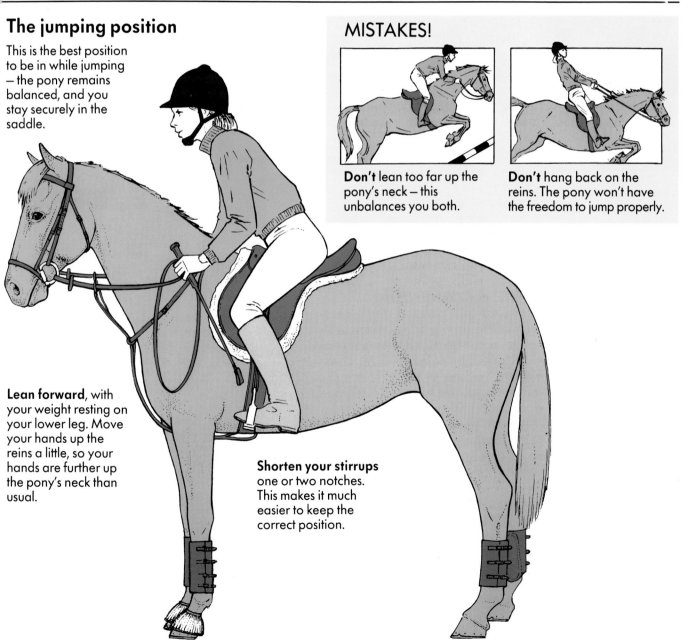

MISTAKES!

Don't lean too far up the pony's neck — this unbalances you both.

Don't hang back on the reins. The pony won't have the freedom to jump properly.

Lean forward, with your weight resting on your lower leg. Move your hands up the reins a little, so your hands are further up the pony's neck than usual.

Shorten your stirrups one or two notches. This makes it much easier to keep the correct position.

Jumping small fences

Trotting over a line of poles is the second step toward jumping. After this you can add a small jump to the end of the row.

Re-positioning the poles

Once the pony picks up his feet over the poles in walk you can try trotting over them. For this you have to re-position the poles – start with three or four about 130cm (52in) apart.

Go over the poles, lengthening and shortening the distance until your pony can trot over them in an easy rhythm, without having to stretch or shorten his stride awkwardly.

When you are confident in this pace, and used to the rise you get when the pony goes over the pole, you're ready to jump a low fence.

Basic jumps

To make your first jump, you need something to lift the poles off the ground. If you don't have any jump stands, use a pair of milk crates, oil drums or even upturned buckets.

The jump need only be a few centimetres high at this stage. The best fence to start with is a cross-pole. This consists of two overlapping poles – one raised at the left and the other raised at the right.

Aim for the centre of the cross – it is the lowest part of the jump and it teaches the pony to jump straight. Keep the centre point about 15cm (6in) high.

Using a cross-pole

There are two ways of using this small jump. One way is to have the cross-pole on its own. The other is to have three or four trotting poles before the jump. Either method can work well – just compare the two ways and decide which would suit you best:

If your pony stays well-behaved and calm, jumping over a single cross-pole is an easy way to start jumping. Remember to approach in a straight line and at an active trot – exactly the same as for trotting poles.

Using trotting poles before the jump makes sure your pony keeps a steady rhythm up to the cross-pole. If he tends to rush a bit then trotting-pole practice will keep him calm.

You need someone on the ground to straighten the line of poles if the pony knocks one of them. It's always best to

have at least one other person around when you're practising, otherwise you spend more time adjusting the jumps than you do going over them!

Jumping position

Having practised the jumping position, you can now put it to full use. Go into forward position as you approach the fence, taking hold of the neck strap or a

knee rolls

SADDLE COMFORT
A general-purpose saddle, with knee rolls – the raised bump at the front of the saddle flaps – is safe and comfortable when you start jumping.

There is no need at this stage to use a forward-cut jumping saddle, but if the flaps are straight with nothing to tuck your knees into, you will have to work harder on your balance!

DID YOU KNOW?
When a horse clears a jump correctly the shape he makes is called a *bascule*. The horse has a rounded back, an extended head and neck and his legs tuck up neatly underneath him. This way the horse goes over a jump with the minimum of effort and strain.

handful of mane. Tell yourself – look up, ride forward, lean forward, heels down! Keep repeating these commands to yourself and you will find it helps you as you go over the jump.

The next stage

Now think about using the jump as part of your schooling plan. Try riding a circle, going into a straight line over the jump and then riding forward to a circle again. Circles before and after jumping keep the pony's mind occupied and are good preparation for riding a course.

Circles are also an excellent way of keeping the pony's rhythm and speed even. You can only be sure of a smooth jump from a calm approach.

Ride your circle in an active trot – but don't worry if your pony breaks into

▼ **Trotting poles** are great practice for jumping. The movement of the pony over each pole prepares you for small fences.

► **A cross-pole** is a good fence to start jumping over – the low centre gives you and the pony a point to aim for.

❗ OIL-DRUM SAFETY
● If you use oil drums (barrels) for jumps at home, take great care.
☐ DO wedge drums used on their sides with pegs or lumps of mud.
☐ DO place the poles against the ridges on the drums to stop them rolling off.
☐ DON'T use rusty drums – the metal becomes brittle and dangerous.
☐ DON'T use barrels that have contained poisonous chemicals.
☐ DON'T use barrels upright – the diagrams show how insecure the poles are.

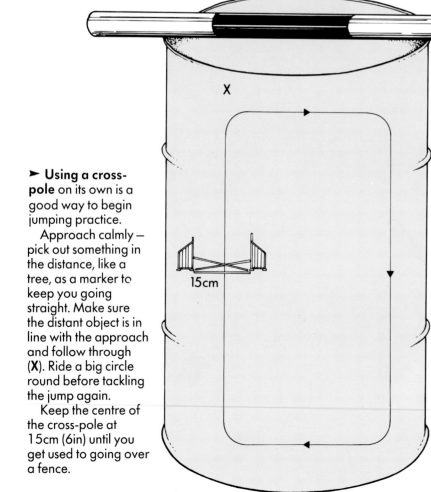

X

15cm

► **Using a cross-pole** on its own is a good way to begin jumping practice.
   Approach calmly – pick out something in the distance, like a tree, as a marker to keep you going straight. Make sure the distant object is in line with the approach and follow through (**X**). Ride a big circle round before tackling the jump again.
   Keep the centre of the cross-pole at 15cm (6in) until you get used to going over a fence.

canter just before take off. You will be jumping from canter soon so this is good practice. If your pony goes too fast afterwards, the second circle will slow him down.

A small course of jumps
As your balance and confidence improve you could make a small course. If you can, arrange a jumping lesson in an indoor school, a small well-fenced paddock or an outdoor arena.

With your instructor's help, plan the course carefully to avoid sharp turns and either very short or very long approaches. The best way to start is by building a line: two or three low jumps of the height you are used to down a long side of the arena.

You will need help to gauge the distance between them. For one non-jumping stride, it should be between 4.5–6.3m (15–21ft) depending on the size of your pony. Make the last jump about 23cm (9in) high.

Letting go of the reins
By moving along the open side of the jumps as you go over, your instructor can make sure your pony stays straight and goes forward. If you feel confident

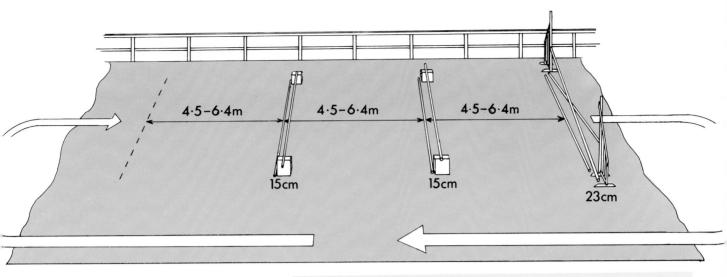

4.5–6.4m 4.5–6.4m 4.5–6.4m

15cm 15cm 23cm

▲ Build a line containing several jumps, once you have mastered one jump of about 15cm (6in). At first, do this with the help of an experienced person. An ideal practice line consists of several small jumps placed against the fence on the long side of the school. Take great care in spacing the jumps out. The distance between them will be 4.5–6.3m (15–21ft). The exact space depends on the size of your pony: a small pony needs less stride space than a larger one. Keep the jumps quite low — the first few at the height you are used to, the last one about 23–30cm (9–12in).

MISTAKES!

Don't look down! Look ahead to the next jump and think about your follow through.

Don't hunch up — your position means the pony must strain to get his quarters over the jump.

enough, now is the time to knot your reins and let go all together. The mane or neck strap are quite close if you need to grab at the last minute.

Although holding the mane makes you feel safe, the aim of the exercise is to be well-balanced enough not to need to hold on. Keep your hands in 'rein position', but don't pull on the reins and put your pony off jumping. If your reins are knotted, you can quietly pick them up to regain control before you come near a corner.

Inviting jumps

When you build jumps, however small they are, remember to make them look inviting. Ponies don't like flappy things like sacks, especially plastic ones that catch the light.

They are put off by jumps which slant toward the take-off side, leaving the high point of the slope nearest the pony. Also, they dislike flimsy-looking jumps without a ground line on the take-off side to guide them.

Rest another pole against the jump stands — but on the ground — to help the pony judge the height. And use cones to fill in the fence — the more solid the jump the better.

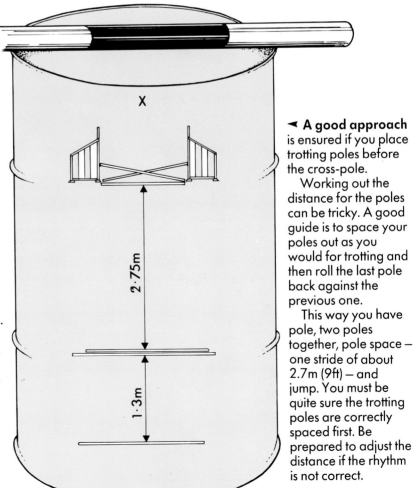

X

2.75m

1.3m

◄ A good approach is ensured if you place trotting poles before the cross-pole.

Working out the distance for the poles can be tricky. A good guide is to space your poles out as you would for trotting and then roll the last pole back against the previous one.

This way you have pole, two poles together, pole space — one stride of about 2.7m (9ft) — and jump. You must be quite sure the trotting poles are correctly spaced first. Be prepared to adjust the distance if the rhythm is not correct.

Jumping combinations

Combination fences are two or more jumps at related distances. This means the horse has to take a set number of strides between the jumps to arrive at the correct take-off point. If there are no strides, or only one or two, between fences then these are jumped 'in combination'.

Judging the distance

All except very novice competitions use combinations as a test of ability of both horse and rider, so training at home is vital to success.

If you have never jumped a combination before, keep it simple and straightforward at first. There is no-thing to be gained from pushing yourself so hard that you force an error. Jumping is challenging but must never be frightening or off-putting for the pony. Later on, you may wish to jump a line of six fences, but start with two!

Using two pairs of stands to build two simple uprights, position them for one 'non-jumping' stride between the two elements. This varies from pony to pony but as a rough guide, for a forward-going mount, allow 2.44-2.74m (8-9ft) for a 12-hand pony, 2.74-3.05m (9-10ft) for a 13-hand pony, and 3.05-3.35m (10-11ft) for a 14-hand pony.

This is the distance between *landing* and *take off*. While your jumps are

small, the *total* distance between the elements is about 4.27-4.88m (14-16ft) for a 12-hand pony, 4.57-5.49m (15-18ft) for a 13-hand pony, and 4.88-6.10m (16-20ft) for a 14-hand pony.

It is important to get the distance as comfortable as possible for both of you, so think about the following points. Is your pony lazy or forward going? Does he have short or long strides? Is the going heavy? If so, this shortens his stride. Has he jumped a double before? If so, he may jump on a longer stride.

Your first double

When you've thought it all out and you think you have worked out the best distance, place the poles on the ground between the stands. Remember to remove the jump cups.

Take your pony over the poles in a steady, active canter. Ride the approach exactly as you would for a simple jump, placing him as well as you can at the first. Even a pole on the ground gives you the feel of jumping. Count to yourself – jump, stride, jump! If it feels smooth, your distance is right and you can start to build a real jump.

Raise the second pole first, about 30-45cm (12-18in). Your pony should quickly settle into a rhythm and jump better as he gains in confidence. Ride forward on the stride between the poles.

▼ **For the well-trained pony** with a thinking rider, combination fences should present no problems on a carefully designed course. Include combination fences in your training courses at home, so your pony takes them in his stride at competitions.

Jumping your first combination

▲ **Position two poles** with one non-jumping stride between them. Ride actively over them, counting in your head 'jump – stride – jump'.

▲ **Lift the second pole** up to about 30-45cm (12-18in). Canter over the first pole, push on in

▼ **When you've practised** jumping *low* combinations, try it with no hands! Not only does this improve your riding, but it also lets the pony lower his head and lift his back into the correct arc shape (bascule).

When you feel ready, raise the first pole to the same height – and you have your first combination! If at any stage the distance feels wrong, then change it straight away.

Most ponies jump on a longer stride as they loosen up and gain experience. Always raise the height of the second element before you alter the first, because this encourages your pony to use himself correctly and not to 'dive' over the jumps.

Improving your riding

Riding combinations gives you a good opportunity to improve your own balance and position. Once you have placed your pony at the first part, he places *himself* at the second, as long as you keep to a straight line from your approach. With experience you get to know exactly when he is going to take off.

Make sure you are allowing the pony complete freedom in his head and neck, and that your lower leg position is secure. If you build a line of three or four low fences into a 'jumping lane' (preferably against the side of an arena) you may feel brave enough to let go of the reins completely.

Jumping with total freedom gives your pony a perfect opportunity to develop his ability. It may be a shock to you the first time the pony really lowers his head and lifts his back in a correct bascule. The feeling is a little like riding a headless pony, but you soon get used to it with practice!

the non-jumping stride and let the pony enjoy popping over the second element.

▲ **Once you are jumping smoothly,** put the first pole up to the height of the second element — and canter over your first combination.

Placing pole

Placing poles are normally used in trot, when it is easier to judge a pony's stride, rather than in canter. But if you have difficulty in 'seeing' a stride, position a pole on the ground on the last stride before take off.

By now, you should have a better idea of the length of your pony's stride. This is the distance you should place the pole from the base of the jump. So if your pony's canter stride is about 3m (10ft) long, then put the placing pole 3m (10ft) from the jump. Approach in an active, bouncy canter and ride forward to meet the pole. This should give you a perfect take off and help you to overcome any problems of placing for the jump.

▼ **By varying** the number of strides between elements and altering the height and shape of the jumps, you both develop scope and confidence.

Your first course

After working on a line of fences and building up confidence by doing plenty of gridwork, it's time to move on to a basic jumping course. A course gives you the chance to put your gridwork exercises into practice and to learn how to ride and turn *between* jumps.

The right approach

The main difference between gridwork and riding a course is that you now need to change directions (change rein) as well as keep your rhythm and balance. This should not present any problems: the aids are the same as for turning left or right on the flat.

So, before you try your first course, take time to think about all you have learned so far. Your approach to a fence is critical. There is no excuse for 'cutting corners': aim for straight lines before *and after* the fence. Your gridwork helps with this but it's easy to get excited and forget everything you've been practising when the crunch comes!

Forward planning

Start by warming up on the flat, then practise over one fence or combination before putting them together as a course. This gives you time to make sure that the pony is moving well – obedient to your aids – and to get yourself settled

▼ **Jumping low fences** is an important part of training at all levels. When you're learning, clearing a small jump in good style increases your confidence. And, when you're more experienced, practice fences provide a good warm-up exercise.

and 'in the mood' for jumping.

When the course is built, the fences will be much the same as you have used in your gridwork and no more than about 60cm (2ft) high and 90cm (3ft) wide. Take a good look at the jumps and check which are uprights and which are spreads. In a trotting exercise, the instructor may make things easier by putting a placing pole 2.5-3m (8-9ft) in front of upright jumps so the pony arrives correctly. (Placing poles are not used when jumping out of canter.)

Otherwise, don't worry too much about the distances between each fence. Instead, concentrate on the course itself – the changes of rein and position of the

jumps. You can then think about how to ride them.

Spread fences, with height *and* width, may look daunting but are usually quite straightforward. They may be 'ascending oxers' – double or triple bars which are lower at the front than the back; 'oxers' (true parallels); or, perhaps, descending oxers which help the horse to land well clear of the fence.

An ascending spread fence is probably the most inviting for a horse, especially if arranged as ascending cross-poles. These not only make the horse go straight but also encourage him to pick his feet up. Remember to keep the rhythm and balance, to ride the horse

★ **TWO-IN-ONE**
To make a course more interesting, build a combination jump. Combinations consist of two or three obstacles placed one after the other with one or two non-jumping strides between.

straight and to look *beyond* the fence.

If you try to rush things, the horse will either get too close and not be able to gain enough height, or he may take off too early and make a huge jump which is unnecessary – and uncomfortable for you! Just stay with the horse and let him reach forward and down with his head and neck.

Be ready to take up the reins again on landing and to help the horse keep his balance so he can make a good approach to the next fence.

Upright fences need a careful approach. The horse has to stand off so that he can drive forward and up off his hocks. For fences no more than about 60cm (2ft) high, keep your legs close to the horse to encourage forward movement and hold him straight. He can then take the jumps in his stride.

Typical uprights are made of poles with 'fillers' such as straw bales or greenery; gates; walls and planks. A single pole can also be filled in with diagonal poles to make it more solid.

Keeping control

All too often riders are so relieved to have jumped a fence that they collapse in a heap on the other side, allowing the horse to stop completely or wobble off track. Now that you are on a proper course, you must think about the next fence and not look back to see whether you have cleared the last one.

Do not be tempted to sit like too much of a passenger – the pony may simply refuse or run out. This is particularly important when you have a double combination fence. You must gather your reins up quickly on landing from the first part, then sit up and kick on. If you are not riding forward, many horses run out of steam and, if you are not riding straight, the pony will almost certainly run out at the second part. A steady rhythm is important too: if a horse rushes his fences, he will flatten over the jump and may knock it down.

Finally – and very important – remember to give your pony a big thank you when he's jumped well.

THE BOX GRID
It's a good idea to use cross-poles for your first course (opposite). Then you can get used to the changes of direction without having to worry about the fences themselves.

▼ **A cross-pole fence** is found at all levels. Here a group of eventing competitors use it to prepare for the cross-country section.

Your first course

The most adaptable small course is a box-type grid of four fences making two double combinations with a change of direction. Once you can cope with low cross-poles, adjust them to make higher uprights and ascending spreads. You can also add more fences outside the basic square layout as you gain confidence.

The distance between the fences of each combination should be 9-10m (30-33ft) for two non-jumping strides and 6-6.3m (20-21ft) for one stride.

Riding a box-type grid

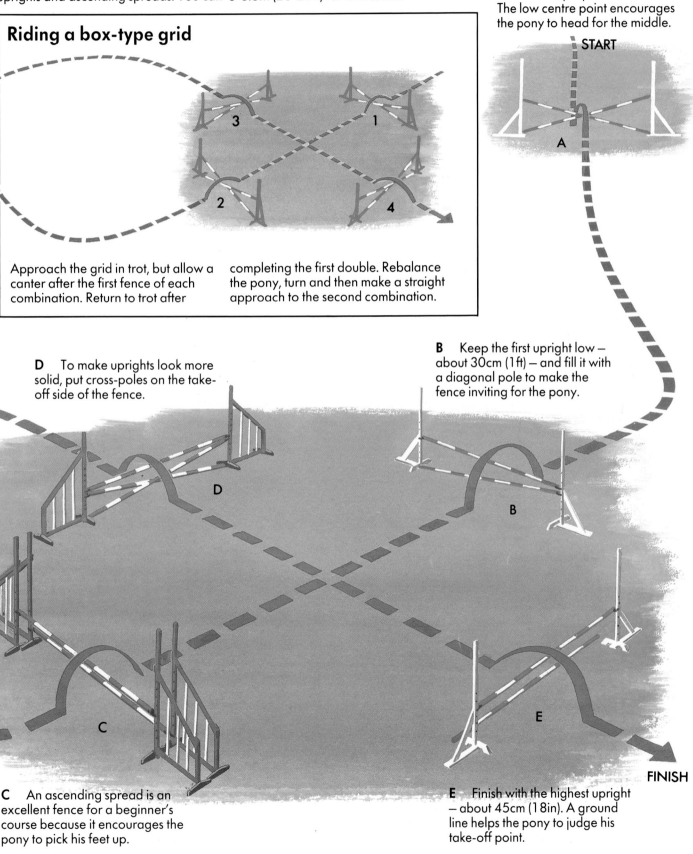

Approach the grid in trot, but allow a canter after the first fence of each combination. Return to trot after completing the first double. Rebalance the pony, turn and then make a straight approach to the second combination.

A A cross-pole fence is a suitable first jump for a course. The low centre point encourages the pony to head for the middle.

D To make uprights look more solid, put cross-poles on the take-off side of the fence.

B Keep the first upright low – about 30cm (1ft) – and fill it with a diagonal pole to make the fence inviting for the pony.

C An ascending spread is an excellent fence for a beginner's course because it encourages the pony to pick his feet up.

E Finish with the highest upright – about 45cm (18in). A ground line helps the pony to judge his take-off point.

Practice jumping course: 1

Jumping over a series of fences – rather than just a single obstacle – encourages you to ride accurately and helps to improve your balance. A carefully designed course prepares you for show-jumping competitions and can be great fun for the pony as well.

Planning a course

If possible, use a level area for your practice jumping. This makes it easier to judge the distances between fences and helps the pony to keep his footing.

On uneven ground, think carefully about where to place the jumps and avoid any sudden or awkward turns. Walk round the area, making a rough drawing of it with notes about any difficult areas.

With your rough sketch handy, you can map out a more detailed course at home: planning it on paper is much easier than trying to arrange the fences at the start of your practice session. Decide what kinds of jump you want to include and think about the distances between them. Make sure that the fences are not too close to the boundary wall or hedge.

The ideal course

The ideal course consists of a mixture of uprights (jumps with height but no width) and spreads (jumps with width as well as height). Start with a course of four or five jumps and keep them no higher than 60cm (2ft) so that you can concentrate on improving your riding skills rather than worrying about clearing big obstacles.

Begin your course with a very simple jump to encourage your pony and get you both settled. Also try to include at least one turn so you change rein.

Two spread fences placed one after the other encourage a horse to stretch and to use his neck and back correctly. He spends longer in the air so it also gives you time to think about your jumping position.

If you ride at a school, look at the kinds of course your instructors build and talk to them about your own ideas. You can also compare plans with other riders and pit your jumping skills against one another. Try asking your instructor if you can build a course during the lesson – it makes a pleasant change for everyone.

CHECKPOINT
Bear in mind the following tips when you practise jumping.

Ride directly towards all fences keeping a steady rhythm.

Make low jumps at first – no higher than 60cm (2ft).

Use spread fences (both height and width) as well as uprights.

◄ **Competition jumping** is often one of the highlights of the horse-lover's day. You can prepare both yourself and your pony over practice courses at a riding school or at home.

! CAVALLETTI
● Many riding schools use cavalletti (poles attached to crosses) which can be turned over to vary the height from about 15-45cm (6-18in).

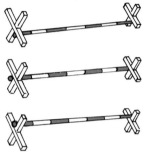

They must be used carefully and *never* stacked. Because the pole is bolted to the cross, it remains upright when knocked. It can therefore become a dangerous obstacle if the pony falls and gets his legs caught.

★ ALTERNATIVES
Plastic Bloks are a good alternative to cavalletti. These have notches at different heights to secure a pole and, being light and not fixed, the pole falls to the ground when knocked. Otherwise you can make your own jumps by placing poles on oil drums or beer crates.

Successful jumping

Before you start jumping, it's important to spend some time letting the pony warm up. Allow about 15 minutes for schooling your pony.

Walk the course on foot and plot where you are going to make turns. Apart from improving the way you ride, it's good preparation for competitive events – walking the course is essential at all levels of show jumping.

If the pony can't be left safely, 'walk' the course on horseback. Once you know the course well you can concentrate on your riding technique rather than worrying about your route over uneven ground or difficult fences and turns.

When you start, keep the session short: 20 minutes is enough. Remember, your pony is having to do all the work and, even if you want to keep going, he's probably tired!

You can also make it more enjoyable for the pony if you change the route around your course during a session. This will keep him interested. It also prevents the ground from becoming too hoof-trodden.

Always end the session on a good note, when your pony has just jumped well. Then walk around quietly for about 15 minutes to let him 'cool off'.

Riding technique

Riding positively and concentrating on the job in hand are particularly import-ant when you're jumping. If you're keen, the pony will be too.

Spaces between jumps

Non-jumping strides are the paces a horse takes between landing over one fence and taking off for the next. If there are more than three strides between fences, the horse can work out the distance for himself. But with several fences close to one another, you need to help him measure his stride. The length of a horse's stride varies according to its height and build. These figures give you a guideline to the distances required between jumps:

	Ponies	Horses
One stride		
trot	6.3m (21ft)	7.2m (24ft)
canter	7.2m (24ft)	7.8m (26ft)
Two strides		
trot	9m (30ft)	10.2m (34ft)
canter	10.2m (34ft)	10.8m (36ft)
Three strides		
trot	13.2m (44ft)	13.8m (46ft)
canter	13.8m (46ft)	14.4m (48ft)

Ideally, take a friend with you to pick up fallen poles and alter any fences so you don't have to dismount and disturb your pony.

Look ahead of you all the time, so that you can gauge exactly how far to ride before beginning to turn. Even if you hear a pole rattle behind you, don't be tempted to look back.

Ride straight towards the centre of

Upright and spread fences

basic upright

cross poles

basic spread

Uprights and spreads consist of one or more poles suspended by posts or barrels at either end.
● A basic upright consists of a single pole suspended at either end.
● Crossing two poles makes an ideal practice jump – good for you and the pony.
A cross-pole fence encourages you to ride

directly towards the centre and, at the same time, the high sides remind your pony to tuck his feet up and out of the way of the poles.
● Spread fences are made up of two or more poles placed alongside each other. Always position spreads with a straight run up to them so that the pony has time to see the fence clearly.

◄ **To avoid disturbing** your pony's rhythm during jumping sessions, ask a friend to pick up any poles you knock over.

each fence. If you attempt to jump at an angle, your pony may run out or refuse.

When you are jumping at a canter, make sure that the pony is on the correct leg for the direction you want to turn. (The inside leg should always lead on a turn or the pony could trip up.)

Most ponies will change naturally to the correct leg while in the air over a jump. If it's wrong, don't panic. Return

to a trot, ride a circle if necessary, and then ask for the canter again. Although you would gain penalties for circling in a competition, give your pony every chance during practice sessions.

Try to create an even speed before and after each jump so that your pony can build up a steady rhythm. The paces between the fences can be more of a challenge than the jumps themselves!

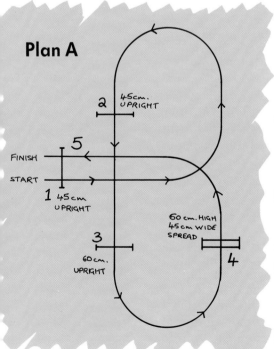

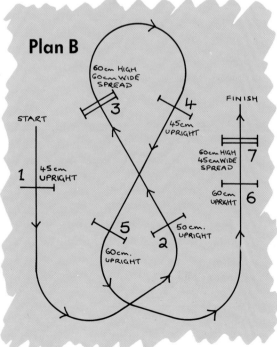

Plan A: An ideal practice course for the beginner. Low jumps increase your confidence. Include at least one spread to improve your jumping position and to encourage the pony to stretch his neck and back.

Plan B: A figure-of-eight course with a variety of jumps extends the skill and agility of both horse and rider. Always begin the course with the easiest jump to get you both off to a good start, and go on to progressively harder fences.

Practice jumping course: 2

Types of spread fence

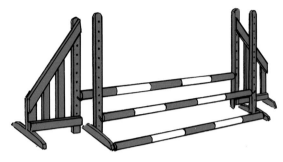

▲ **An ascending spread** has two or more poles which get progressively higher. Always approach this jump from the front with the poles sloping away from you.

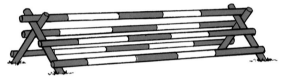

▲ **A pyramid fence** has at least three poles, the highest in the middle and two lower ones either side. It is particularly useful during practice sessions because you can jump it from either direction.

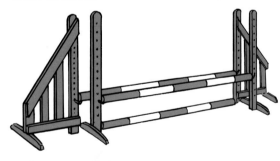

▲ **A true parallel**, with two top poles of the same height, is the most challenging spread of all. Because the pony makes an arc to jump clear you may feel you are jumping an even higher fence!

▶ **A spread that ascends** is inviting and encourages a pony to stretch his neck as he clears its height and width. Notice how the rider's forward position helps the horse to jump boldly, and that both horse and rider are looking ahead to the next fence.

Experimenting with different types of fences can make your jumping course much more interesting. It also stands you in good stead when you enter show-jumping competitions.

Spread fences

It is important that you're familiar with the types of fences you are likely to come across. Unlike uprights, spread fences come in all shapes and sizes. You need to approach each one in a particular way to give your pony the best chance.

An ascending spread is made up of a series of poles that slope upward and away from you. The front pole should be a few centimetres from the ground and the back pole at a height of about 60cm (2ft) to begin with. You can increase the height to 90cm (3ft) or more as you gain confidence. Always jump this fence from the front because the pony cannot see its spread properly from the other side.

The ascending spread is an easy and inviting jump. Ride on at it and really let your pony stretch. You should get used to the feel of your hands following foward as the pony stretches out his head to clear the width *and* the height.

A pyramid fence is made up of horizontal poles built up into a triangular-shaped jump. Always position the middle pole higher than the back and front poles to create a pyramid shape. Such fences are ideal for a practice course because you can take them from either direction. As a result, you can change your route without altering the jump.

A pyramid fence encourages your pony to lift and round his back more because the centre of the jump is the highest point. Approach this jump from a canter.

A true parallel has two top poles of equal height. A pony may find it difficult to judge how wide he has to jump because he cannot see the back pole. To get your pony used to it, lower the front pole slightly so that the second pole is just visible.

This fence encourages the roundest jump from your pony because of its spread. The pony should make an arc to clear both poles. It is important to get your speed right. If you take the fence too fast, the front pole is quite likely to get knocked down. If you approach too slowly your pony may not manage to jump clear and the back pole may fall.

The ground line

The pony needs to judge the height of the fence so that he knows where to take off. To do this he focuses his eyes on the top and bottom of an obstacle.

Fences over 60cm (2ft) are easier to clear if there is a ground line. This can be a pole laid on the ground or a filler.

If you use a pole as a ground line, place it on the ground directly below the front pole and make sure it cannot roll. Never place a ground line behind the front pole as the pony will not be able to judge his take-off point correctly.

Fillers under either upright or spread fences also help your pony. These can be made out of cones, oil drums, bundles of brushwood or you can buy purpose-built fillers. The pony sees most clearly if you block out as much daylight as possible.

Judging a pony's stride

The length of a pony's stride varies enormously. With fences following closely one after the other, it helps to know how many strides your pony takes between them at a canter.

Mark two points 40m (44yd) apart in a jumping paddock. Canter between these points from both directions at slightly different speeds and count the strides.

The three plans on these pages are a guide to help you plan your own courses. You can adapt them to suit your needs and the jumping area where you practise. Once you have worked out how long your pony's strides are at a particular speed, you'll be able to decide exactly where to position the jumps.

Plan A

Plan A uses all types of fences. You can jump the uprights and the pyramid from either direction, so you can vary the course without moving the jumps. The parallel and ascending spread, however, must be jumped from the front.

Notice that the first jump is simple and faces toward the gate leading 'home' – encouraging the pony forward.

There are plenty of strides between fences to give the pony time to prepare for each jump. This is particularly important when going from a spread to an upright (fences 3 and 4) because spreads require longer strides while, for an upright, you need to check your speed.

The largest and most tricky fence comes last so that you can jump this when you have warmed up.

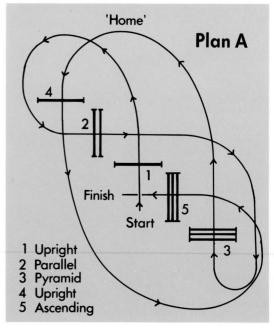

Plan A

1 Upright
2 Parallel
3 Pyramid
4 Upright
5 Ascending

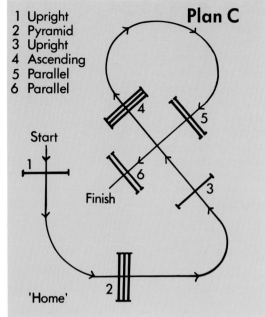

1 Upright
2 Pyramid
3 Upright
4 Ascending
5 Parallel
6 Parallel

Plan C

Plan C

Plan C presents a real challenge. The positioning of the fences is more tricky and you have to think about the pony's strides. However, the first jump is fairly straightforward and again faces toward 'home'.

The second fence must be inviting as it is turning away from home.

Ride strongly but carefully over the upright and push on to the spread.

Allow yourself plenty of room when you turn to the last two parallels as this helps steady your pony's speed.

When facing home, your pony may want to hurry. Do not let him rush too much. The last fence – a large parallel – is the most challenging on this course and you will need time to judge your approach.

Plan B

Plan B is a good layout for a small area as all turns are outside the fences – the jumps themselves occupy little space.

It starts off with an easy upright, which faces toward home as before.

Circle widely between fences, especially before approaching the last two fences. This allows the pony to approach at the right speed.

Unlike the first two plans, this course ends with a close-set double – two fences placed one after the other with one non-jumping stride between. Decide how much you need to push on between fences *before* tackling the course.

The average distance for a non-jumping stride between small fences is about 6m (18-21ft). Adjust the distances to suit your pony's stride.

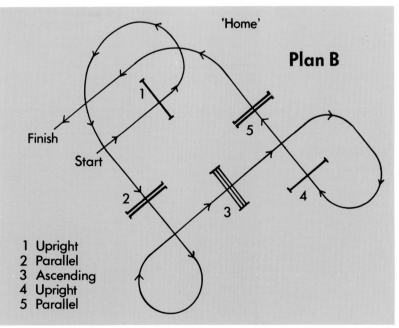

'Home'

Plan B

Finish

Start

1 Upright
2 Parallel
3 Ascending
4 Upright
5 Parallel

Practice jumping course: 3

➤ **Painting your poles** makes them look like proper show jumps, and means that your pony is accustomed to brightly coloured fences when he sees them at competitions. The paint also protects your poles from the weather.

★ **THE BLOK**
As an alternative to – or as well as – making jumps, you could buy the specially made plastic Bloks. These can be used as both stands and fillers to build any type of jump you like.

Each Blok has grooves for poles at different heights, and they can be safely stacked.

A course built from home-made jumps can be every bit as challenging and varied as a professionally designed circuit. You should be able to collect enough different objects to build any kind of fence you like – as long as all your materials are solid and sturdy.

Show-jumping poles

You may be able to find some second-hand or unpainted poles by looking in your local paper. If not, ask at the nearest branch of the Pony Club or your riding club. Home-made poles must be free of dangerous projections like nails or broken ends of wood. For instance, fallen branches need careful trimming before they are safe to use as poles. Offcuts of wood from a builder's yard may be suitable for making poles, but you must have the sharp, square edges rounded off.

A coat of paint brightens up your poles (or pole substitutes) and makes them look much more professional. This also means that your pony gets used to painted fences before he sees them in the ring. Go for any bright colour and contrast it with bands of white. It is this contrast that can make show jumps look alarming to an unsuspecting pony.

Remember that the poles may get knocked around quite a bit so use gloss paint over several layers of undercoat. If your jumps are going to be kept outside in all weathers, this makes them last longer and stops them rotting.

Jump stands

Jump stands can be quite easy to make, remembering again that they must be solid and not fall down too easily. A single piece of upright timber, 7.5–10cm (3–4in) square, mounted on a solid base, can have holes drilled at 7.5cm (3in) intervals to take jump cups.

Jump cups can be made at home by DIY enthusiasts. The cup is carved in a block of wood, a minimum of 5cm (2in) wide, and the edges *rounded off* with sandpaper. A wooden peg is attached to the block for slotting through the holes in the stand.

Your poles should never be fixed or nailed to the jump stands. They should be resting in cups (professional or home-made). A jump that looks as though it could be knocked down but is actually fixed in place by the stand can cause a very nasty fall. Always place poles on the far side of the stand so that they fall down if your pony knocks them with his legs. Also, never leave 'spare' jump cups jutting out from the stands.

Old car tyres laid flat on the ground make good jump stands as well. You can easily alter the height by adding or taking away a tyre from your stack and there is no need to use a saw or hammer and nails!

Fillers

Your jumps will be much more inviting to your pony if they have a ground line and/or fillers. This makes it easier for the pony to judge the height of the fence

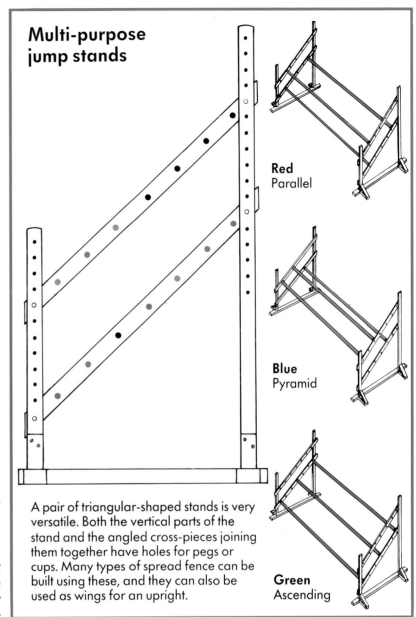

Multi-purpose jump stands

Red Parallel

Blue Pyramid

Green Ascending

A pair of triangular-shaped stands is very versatile. Both the vertical parts of the stand and the angled cross-pieces joining them together have holes for pegs or cups. Many types of spread fence can be built using these, and they can also be used as wings for an upright.

◄ **Jumping a variety** of sizes and shapes keeps you and your pony on your toes and prepares you for show-jumping obstacles.

Be imaginative and change the jumps around frequently so that both of you stay alert.

and where to take off. Tyres make good fillers as well as stands, and are very safe should your pony crash into them by mistake.

Straw bales make useful fillers, but they have one dangerous drawback – the string holding them together. If your pony gets his feet caught in the strings he will be very frightened and may injure himself. To be safe, put the bales inside a sack or wrap them up in a pair of old curtains. Make sure the edges are well tucked in to avoid unexpected flapping in the breeze just when you want to jump!

Wooden pallets are useful too. These are platforms used for lifting and stacking goods; you may be able to obtain some from a local feed merchant or factory warehouse. Only use them if they are solidly made and in good condition. If the wood is very lightweight they break easily leaving jagged edges, and the nails holding them together can work loose.

Purpose-built cones also make excellent fillers. They are light, easy to move around and fill in the gap in fairly low jumps.

Home jumping course

This course uses up very little space. Having your jumps together in a block makes it easier to swap things around. It also leaves more of the paddock free to mark out a schooling area.

Make the first jump easy, encouraging and facing toward 'home' (usually the gate). As you land you should be looking toward the next jump and planning your approach. There is plenty of room to turn for the next jump as long as you use the space well. Don't make the second turn until you can see the approach line. Cutting the corner unbalances your pony and makes the jump difficult. This jump should still be inviting but a little higher than the first.

Measure the distance carefully between the two parts of the double and beware of riding too fast. Facing home reassures your pony and he should now be getting well into his stride. The fourth jump is a spread facing away from home, so remember to push on.

The final fence can be the most challenging – toward home again and when both you and your pony feel at your most confident near the finish.

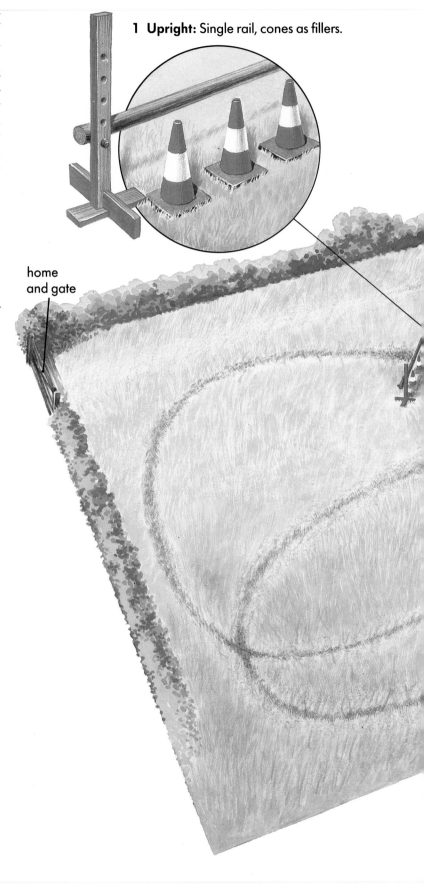

1 Upright: Single rail, cones as fillers.

home and gate

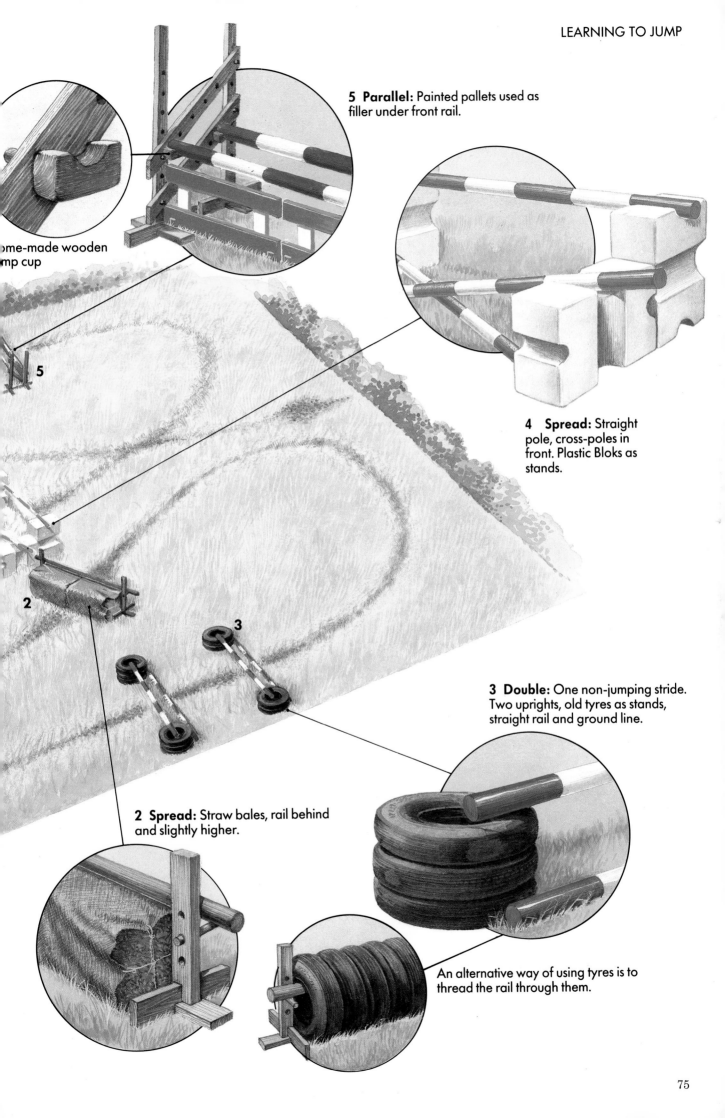

5 Parallel: Painted pallets used as filler under front rail.

ome-made wooden mp cup

5

4 Spread: Straight pole, cross-poles in front. Plastic Bloks as stands.

2

3

3 Double: One non-jumping stride. Two uprights, old tyres as stands, straight rail and ground line.

2 Spread: Straw bales, rail behind and slightly higher.

An alternative way of using tyres is to thread the rail through them.

Jump stands, cups and poles

As well as the traditional wooden jump stands that hold poles in place with jump cups, you can now buy modern ones made of synthetic materials that are safe, versatile and light.

Traditional structures

These consist of a vertical piece of timber, squared off and usually drilled with holes to take the cups. It is supported by a base of either two, three or four 'feet' of wood or, more elaborately, by vertical slats of wood forming a wing.

Some stands need holes for the cups; others have none and the cups can be slid up and down the upright. Cups should be fixed on the landing side of the jump, or else to the inside of the stand. They must never be fixed to the approach side of the jump in case the pony knocks the pole – and pulls over the stand as well.

The cups should be shallow enough so that the poles fall if definitely hit, but not so shallow that they are dislodged at the slightest touch and unmounted friends are forever having to put the jump together again.

Modern stands

Modern polythene and polystyrene jump stands, such as Bloks and Tri-Jumps, are a safe alternative to cavalletti. They are shaped so you can use them in various ways, and you can stack them on top of one another to make different patterns and heights of jump. Light enough to move easily yet stable and secure in use, they are weather resistant without needing to be painted or coated with preservative.

Portajumps, popularly referred to as 'wheelies', are cheap, easily moved stands consisting simply of a single vertical piece of timber with a one-piece, welded cup. The base is a car tyre on its side, which is very sturdy. By tilting the stand slightly you can roll it around to where you want it, so they are excellent for children to set up without adult help. They are used by many Pony Club branches.

Poles

Poles should be round, never square, as these could injure the pony. They are either painted in bright colours striped with white, or unpainted, when they are known as 'rustic'. Unpainted ones need coating with wood preservative or they do not last long.

Poles rest on the cups and are never fixed to the stands, which would be dangerous. Buy the thickest poles you can find, within reason – ponies respect them better and they do not fly about when knocked down, as flimsy ones do.

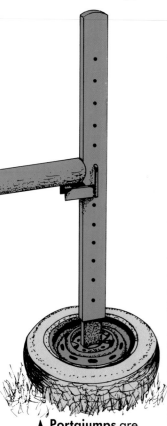

▲ **Portajumps** are convenient and quick to set up. They come in several colours.

▼ **Tri-Jumps** are tough but light and allow for different jump heights.

► **Bloks** also make versatile jump stands. Built from synthetic material, they are secure in use but easy to move around. As with Tri-Jumps, it is safe to stack them.

mprovising jumps

The expensive-looking jumps you see at major competitions can be re-created – with a few basic materials and a little imagination – for your own course.

Safe and sound

Whatever you use to make your jump stands, cups and fillers, always think about their safety. Never use square poles – which can easily hurt a pony – and avoid flimsy-looking hurdles which fly about when knocked down.

Be particularly careful about the kind of fillers you use. Don't use anything that your pony could trip over or get his foot caught in. In general, it's best to avoid improvised metal items – especially corrugated iron or old railings – as sharp or jagged edges are extremely dangerous.

Less obvious hazards include baler twine which can tangle in a pony's legs, rough, splintered timber, and nails sticking out of old pieces of wood.

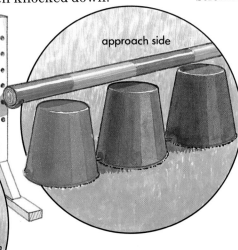

▼ **Plastic tubs with plants** in them create a true 'competition' atmosphere! Half-fill them with sand or soil to anchor the plants.

▲ **Upturned plastic buckets** with the handles removed provide colourful fillers. Don't use metal buckets, as these rust and get jagged edges.

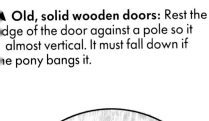

▲ **Old, solid wooden doors:** Rest the edge of the door against a pole so it almost vertical. It must fall down if the pony bangs it.

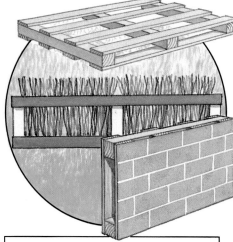

◄ **Wooden pallets** are very versatile. You can make a brush fence by filling them with tightly packed sticks and twigs. Or you can attach sturdy wooden panels to them, and paint them to look like a wall.

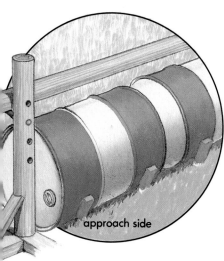

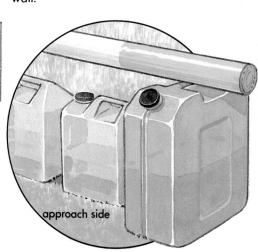

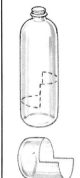

Improvise jump cups using strong plastic bottles. Cut half-way through the bottle, about 4cm (1½in) from the base, then about a third of the way up the bottle to form a cup shape. Nail it to the stand on the far side.

▲ **Oil drums on their sides** can be used as fillers, but you must peg them so they don't roll about when bumped.

Plastic containers: Make sure they are clean and free of all traces of chemicals, then half-fill them with water to make them sturdy.

3 Improve your riding

Polishing your technique

You should now be quite capable of walking, trotting and cantering, and be ready to concentrate on refining your style. The aim is to make your pony listen and respond instantly to your aids, so that riding becomes a secret conversation between the two of you.

Relax and stay supple

Remember the first time you sat on a pony? You were probably tense from top to toe because you didn't know how it would feel when the pony moved! Tension slows down a lazy pony and excites a lively one. Sitting rigidly is also tiring for you and a worn-out rider cannot give efficient aids.

The more at home you feel in the saddle, the more comfortable it is for the pony and the easier it is for you to give quiet, unnoticeable aids.

Keeping your hands and legs still while the pony is moving is the first step. This comes from being able to relax the muscles *not* in use so you sit 'softly' with your pony. There are two areas of your body you should now concentrate on loosening up (but not slumping) – your seat, and your neck and shoulders.

All the time a pony is moving, there is a natural swing to his back, most noticeable in walk, more bouncy in trot, and more rocking in canter. By softening the muscles in your seat, you will find these movements much simpler to follow.

Practise on the lunge

If possible, ask somebody to lunge you

n a quiet pony. Rather than doing rigorous balancing exercises, just practise sitting still for a while. Start in walk. Imagine you have a book balanced on your head and sit up tall, holding your head and shoulders motionless. Now let the pony's movement flow through your seat, hips and lower back, keeping your waist supple.

When you feel good at this stage, cross your stirrups over the front of the saddle, still with the same relaxed position in walk. Knot the reins and let go of them if you feel confident enough. Put your hands on your hips or stretch them out to the side. This makes sure you are not using the reins to balance.

Once you are quite relaxed, try some trotting. You may want to take back your stirrups to begin with. Leave ►

▼ **Make sure your aids** are as gentle as possible, keeping a constant but even contact on both reins. By just closing your fingers on the reins while your legs are still on the pony's sides, you should feel a response.

This horse is performing the counter canter – he is well-balanced and obedient enough to strike off on the wrong leg when asked to do so by his rider.

Accepting the bit

Above the bit means the pony's nose is too high and poked forward.
On the bit means the pony is well balanced, responsive and easy to ride, and his face is on or slightly in front of the vertical.
Behind the bit describes a pony whose nose is tucked in toward his chest. Relax your hands and ride strongly forward.

▲ **Above the bit**

▲ **On the bit**

▲ **Behind the bit**

your reins knotted, but hold on to the saddle if you are bouncing around. Then you are free to concentrate on softening your seat.

Off the lunge

Remember to sit quietly on your pony whenever you ride, not just on the lunge. Once you feel that you are supple and relaxed, try asking your pony to slow down or speed up without changing pace. You may want to lengthen your stirrups a little at the start to help you sit deeper in the saddle.

'On the bit'

Once you've concentrated on your own posture, it's time to think about how the pony carries himself. Any pony works better and is easier to ride when he is 'on the bit'. This means that you and the pony are in full communication: he feels light in your hands so that your rein contact can be gentle while he responds to your leg aids.

The pony should be attentive to you – and not thinking about how much longer he has to plod around the arena or about what is going on in the next field. He should be working actively in response to your legs, and moving with impulsion (energy).

Once you feel in harmony with your pony, you are beginning to learn the real art of riding.

▲ **Once you can sit still**, cross your stirrups and knot your reins. Stretch your hands out to the sides or put them on your hips so you rely on natural balance to keep your position.

► **When you are riding** a pony in walk, the movement in your upper body is exactly the same as it is if you walk on your own two feet. You can practise your balance between rides by walking about with a book balanced on your head. As an added bonus, this improves your posture generally!

▼ **After practice on the lunge,** you should be able to sit more deeply in the saddle.

Check what you know

Whenever riding, always think 'safety first': use the right gear, check your tack, think of your pony and don't try anything new unless you know you can control him.

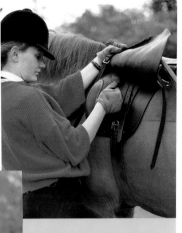

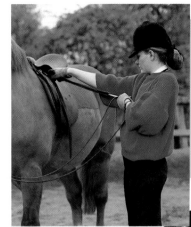

◄ **Check your stirrup** length by putting the knuckles of your right hand on the stirrup bar and lifting the stirrup leather. Hold it against your arm. The iron should reach your armpit.

▲ **Check the girth:** if it needs tightening pull the girth strap up and fasten the buckle a hole or two higher.

◄ **Check your riding** position: an imaginary line should run through shoulder, hip and heel.

► **Warming up gets** you and your pony relaxed and ready for your ride. Always start with walking and then gradually move up the paces.

► **Ending** a schooling session in walk is part of good riding and shows consideration for the pony. He should move freely and energetically.

◄ **For a safe jumping** position, shorten your stirrups one or two notches. Lean forward with your weight on your lower leg and keep looking ahead.

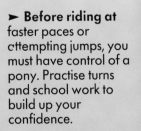

◄ **The correct gear** is not a matter of fashion: a hard hat and sturdy shoes are essential for safe riding.

► **Before riding at** faster paces or attempting jumps, you must have control of a pony. Practise turns and school work to build up your confidence.

Exercises in the arena

Exercises in the arena are an excellent way of consolidating the riding skills you have already learnt. You can improve your control and steering by working in rides and by practising simple turns and circles.

Warming up

When your pony first comes out of the stable, he may be a little stiff. Treat him like an athlete and warm him up gradually at the beginning of a lesson. Walk for several minutes before you start trotting and trot for a while before cantering. There is no rule to say how long you should work in each gait: you must try to 'feel' when your pony is ready to move on.

As a guide, if it is a cold day and your pony is fresh, it is better to trot on earlier. If not, stay in walk until he is moving freely and you can tell he is 'listening' to your aids.

Working in rides

One of the problems of riding in a group is that your pony becomes too automatic. He learns the exercises quickly by copying the other ponies in the class, so he doesn't bother to listen to his rider. Working 'by rides' helps to overcome this. It involves splitting up from the group and riding in opposite directions.

Start by riding in single file up the centre of the arena. The first rider then

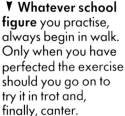

▼ **Whatever school figure** you practise, always begin in walk. Only when you have perfected the exercise should you go on to try it in trot and, finally, canter.

goes left, the second right, the third left and so on. This helps get your pony's attention and also helps you ride to a good rhythm and control the speed of your pony. Imagine the chaos if half the ride went faster than the other half. You could end up with the riding-school equivalent of a motorway pile-up! There is a 'rule' to stop this happening.

When you meet a rider coming toward you, always pass left hand to left hand to avoid collision. This simply means going to the right, leaving the oncoming rider to your left.

Round in circles

When you are happy that your pony is properly warmed up and concentrating

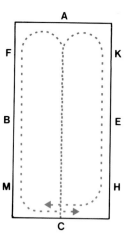

▲ **With several students,** it helps to split the group into two rides. This means everyone has to concentrate – not just follow the leader!

◄ **Riders pass** left hand to left hand.

Riding circles

A standard-sized arena measures 20m (66ft) by 40m (132ft) and is marked out with letters of the alphabet. (See page 135 for an explanation of these letters.) Use these to judge when to change rein.

► **The blue circle** represents a 20m (66ft) circle which uses the full width of the arena. The smaller 15m (50ft) circle, shown in red, requires more accurate control of your pony. **Diagram a** shows how to move into a 15m circle.

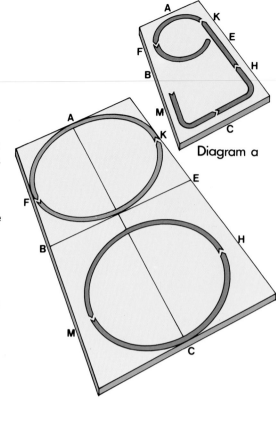

Diagram a

Serpentines

► **A series** of three equally sized loops, made up of half circles – and known as a three-loop serpentine – involves changing both bend and direction. Begin this exercise in walk, and be careful that the loops are not too large or you will run out of space and end up making last-minute adjustments that spoil your balance and rhythm.

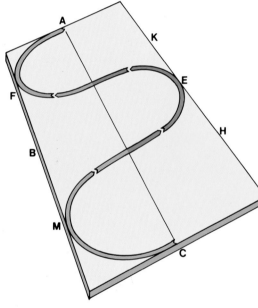

Circles and half circles

► **Once you have mastered** large circles and serpentines, you can practise 10m (33ft) circles, shown in green. Then move on to 10m half circles with a change. These can be ridden with either a short incline (the red version) or a long incline (the blue version). For both, ride a half circle then return to the track on a diagonal.

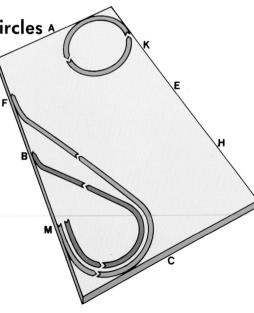

on the work in hand, you can progress to more advanced exercises.

Start off by riding 'large' round the arena, which means all the way around the outside track. Then move on to 20m (66ft) circles. Use half the arena at a time – either at one end or in the middle. Remember that a circle is round, without corners, so you should be riding smoothly and evenly in a regular rhythm.

Whatever you do on one rein, repeat the same exercise on the other rein before moving on to something more difficult. Complete the 20m (66ft) circle on both reins, and in walk and trot, then go on to 15m (50ft) circles.

Changing the rein

Once you and the pony are moving well, you are ready to try riding figures of eight. Changing the rein across the diagonal is not demanding for the pony but is a good test of your control.

Make the two ends of the figure eight the same shape as 20m (66ft) circles. This means that for two or three strides you will be riding across the school on the E-B line through X. This is the time to change the bend, still keeping a smooth, steady rhythm: no quickening! It is a useful suppling exercise and will help you get used to changing your aids from left to right.

You can build up from this exercise to riding a three-loop serpentine. Each loop goes to the side of the arena and is ridden like a half circle. The dressage arena is usually 40m (132ft) long, so this means that each half circle is about 13m (42ft) in diameter.

Improving your skills

The slower your pony moves, the easier it is to make small circles. A 10m (33ft) circle in walk, a 15m (50ft) circle in trot and a 20m (66ft) circle in canter are about the same degree of difficulty. So once you can ride smaller circles in walk, you can ask for smaller circles at faster paces.

Half circles are easier and can be combined with a change of rein – but only in walk and trot to start with. If you can ride a good 15m (50ft) circle in trot, then you should be able to manage a 10m (33ft) half circle and return to the track on a straight diagonal line. Technically, this is called a half circle and change.

Avoiding mistakes

When practising school figures, remember the basic guidelines for turns and circles. Your aids must be applied correctly so that the pony knows what to do. The most common mistakes are caused by riders applying too much rein pressure or the wrong leg aid.

Sensitive hands are important to good riding. With too much *inside* rein, the pony turns his head in and this makes his shoulder fall outward, spoiling the smooth curve you are aiming for. If you apply too much *outside* rein, the opposite happens: the pony has to turn his head out so that his shoulder now falls in on the curve.

Your leg aids are just as important. The pony may try to avoid bending along his length by quickening and shortening his steps and by falling in on the circle or trying to use a bigger circuit. Keep your inside leg against the girth to prevent this. Use your outside leg to keep his quarters in line with the curve.

Finally, keep your hips and shoulders square to the horse's shoulders. If you lean into the circle the horse may do the same and fall in toward the centre.

MAKE YOUR MARK
The letters in a dressage arena give you points to aim for when schooling. You are said to be at a marker as your lower leg passes that point. So, if you wanted to canter at C, for example, your pony should strike off into canter at the moment *you* are next to C rather than your pony's nose or tail.

MISTAKES!

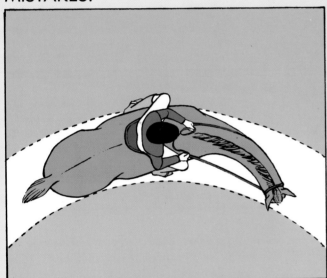

Do not use too much inside rein. This turns the pony's head inward and pushes the off-side shoulder out of line.

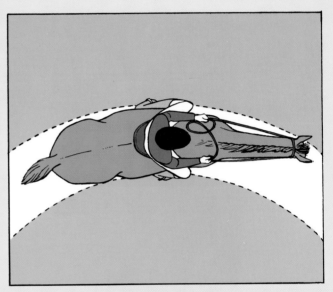

Too much outside rein forces the pony to turn his head outward so that the near-side shoulder falls in on the curve.

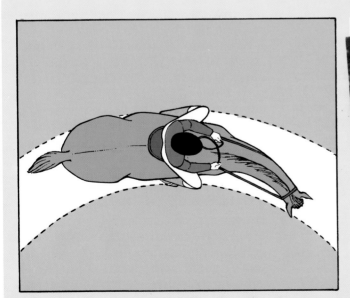

Forgetting to use your outside leg allows the pony to straighten along the spine, so that his quarters fall outward.

▲ **When a horse** is performing a turn successfully, he should have a smooth, even curve throughout the length of his body.

Correct your position

▲ Seeing yourself riding on film is an extremely valuable experience – and can be quite a shock! Sometimes it 'feels' as if you are in the right position when in fact you are not. Look for your good points to build on, and make a list of your faults so you can set about correcting them.

One of the first lessons you learn is how to sit properly in the saddle. It is now time to think in more detail about *why* you sit like this, and how your seat and position affect your pony.

Seat problems

The 'modern' seat has taken many decades to develop. Every aspect has been thought about and improved by experts. The result is that the 'correct' seat is the one that is most effective.

Any faults or weaknesses make the rider less able to get the best from the horse. A bad rider has to work much harder than a good, properly instructed one to achieve the level of success that

he or she would like.

A rider who sits quietly in the saddle doesn't interfere with the pony's movement. Imagine carrying a fidgety, young child on your own back. Then think how much easier it is to give a 'piggy-back' to one who holds on carefully and keeps still.

A sloppy rider gives confused aids, with legs working in different places and hands unsteady on the pony's mouth. Clear, precisely applied aids encourage the pony to listen and be obedient. Such aids are difficult to spot for anyone watching, but the horse is responding.

Some simple faults are easy to understand. A rider with her legs round the horse's shoulders sits heavily on the pony's back, and has to make a great effort to apply a leg aid. A rider tipped forward with legs too far back is unable to use her back and seat. Her legs then have to do extra work to keep the pony active.

The power of thought

Horses are very sensitive to their rider's mood and mental attitude. A calm and gentle rider generally does well on a tense horse, which responds to the calming influence. A tense and aggressive rider upsets some horses, while waking up the lazy ones.

If you have a chance to ride several different types you should soon learn

something about yourself! Try to adapt your mental attitude to suit the horse you are riding. If you are upset and angry about something then you are not in the right frame of mind for schooling, so go for a hack instead.

The same applies if you are very tired or feeling unwell – you won't get the results you would expect on a good day. It is rarely the pony's fault if he doesn't go well.

Filming yourself

Seeing yourself on film is the best way to discover how you really ride. It's easy to think you are doing everything right when in fact a mistake has crept in. If you don't own a video camera, why not rent one for a day or a weekend?

Make the most of the opportunity and work on the flat and over a few jumps. You may be in for a few surprises! Look at your hands – are they steady or do they interfere with the pony's mouth?

Are you tipping forward, rounding your back or hunching your shoulders? Is your back hollow with your hands fixed? Do you react quickly enough when something goes wrong? Do you look good until you ask for a transition

SCHOOLING SESSIONS

Have a purpose clearly in mind when you school your pony. You should aim to have him working quietly but actively forward. He should move with a good outline – on the bit and with his hindlegs under him – and change easily from one pace to another or turn in either direction. He should seem happy and relaxed, yet attentive.

As the pony goes through a schooling session, saliva should appear in the corners of his mouth, which shows that his jaw is relaxed and he is accepting the bit. A dry mouth or lots of froth flying in all directions are both signs of tension or agitation.

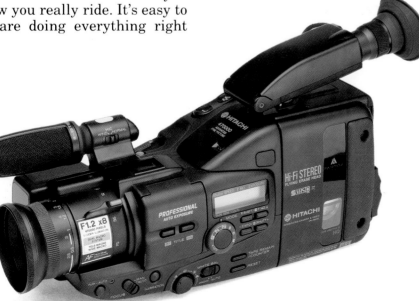

▲ **Why not rent** a video camera for a day or a weekend if you don't own one or can't borrow one? Despite looking complicated, they are quite easy to operate!

to canter, when you suddenly jack-knife forward?

Once you have been critical of yourself (and of your friends!), make a few mental lists. First your good points, which you don't want to lose. Second, the points which you could easily correct now that you are aware of them. Third, the more serious faults which you are going to need help to overcome.

Allot yourselves a period of time – say, four to six weeks – and then have another filming session to see how you have improved.

This makes sure that you really work hard and encourages you when you can tick off some old weaknesses and start a new list to work on.

Looking at others

Start to look critically at other riders – whether at a local show or on the

◄ **Study other riders** at your local riding school, at shows and on television. This gives you an insight into a whole range of different styles and techniques, and their effect on the horse – good or bad!

television. What makes you admire some riders and dislike the style of others?

There are people who appear to be quite the 'wrong' shape to ride well and yet can produce a succession of beautifully schooled horses. There are others who look stunning until the horse moves, when there is immediate tension and discomfort. This is all down to technique and mental attitude. Study the riders closely and see what it is that makes them individual.

Be careful not to copy faults. Few riders are perfect and some get good results in spite of – and not because of – an obvious fault. If you can spot this fault, look very hard for the *good* points as these are the ones to try and copy. You have your own faults and do not need to pick up other people's.

If you can start to think: 'if only he could keep his hands still', or 'if she could ride with more determination', or 'she had a refusal coming up ages before the jump and didn't do anything about it' – then you are beginning to be an educated 'horse person'.

▼ **Thinking positively:** If you don't believe you could possibly jump a particular fence, then it would need a saint of a pony to take you over it.

If you are nervous, your leg and rein aids are affected. By hesitating, you aren't letting the pony go forward – in fact you are virtually telling him not to bother! Alternatively, you may start flapping, and interfere with his stride on the approach to the jump as you attempt to push on. In both cases the pony is likely to refuse – and you to fall off!

▼ Don't ignore problems, even if they seem very minor at first. Nip them in the bud — with professional help if necessary — before they either worsen or lead to other trouble.

Your riding problems solved

Anyone who has ridden for any length of time can tell you that you never stop learning. The more you learn, the more you *want* to learn. As you become more aware of this, you'll find that improving your own riding overcomes all sorts of problems that could otherwise be put down to the pony playing up.

Rooting out problems

A good rider can make an ordinary pony into a very special pony. Whenever you reach a difficult point in your schooling, even day-to-day riding, try asking yourself what you should be doing to improve matters.

Ponies can be wilful or can have great difficulty doing the tasks we ask of them. Remember that the pony didn't ask you to get on his back – it was your choice. This thought helps you to be more sympathetic and patient when things go wrong.

Try not to expect miracles and instant success. Aim for a steady improvement in your work. If you have a problem, don't ignore it. By finding out the cause and the cure, you can prevent a problem becoming so deep rooted that you need a real expert to come and sort it out.

If you truly think your riding and your pony are problem free, then aim for more ambitious training. In this way, you keep learning and your riding is always fun and challenging.

Q

I feel very unsafe when I jump. I keep losing my balance and pulling on the pony's mouth. Can you suggest some tips to help me improve?

A

The first thing is to use a neck strap and hold on to this as you go over the jump. At least then you don't upset the pony. Try to work out *why* you lose your balance. If you keep your heels down and 'fold' well forward from the hips, with your knees tucked firmly into the saddle, you should feel safe.

Try not to tighten up. Remember to look and ride forward before and after the jump, and practise over very small fences. Once you have the 'knack', it seems very easy!

Q

How can I stop myself bumping on the saddle when trotting without stirrups? It's very painful and I can't control my pony properly in the lesson when we have to do this.

A

It sounds as if you are stiffening up and tipping forward, with the result that you bounce on your 'fork'. Start by leaning back slightly (without pulling on the reins) and try to soften your back and seat to follow the swing of the pony's back. Aim to keep the pony to a very slow trot. Whenever you feel uncomfortable, put a finger through the neck strap or under the front arch of the saddle to steady yourself. Once your balance is regained, both you and the pony should feel more comfortable.

Q

Please can you advise me on how to keep my horse 'on the bit'? I seem to achieve it for a little while and then lose it again.

A

Once you have put your horse 'on the bit', ride him more energetically forward from your legs, creating 'impulsion'. In this way he should come lighter and lighter in your hands. By all means correct him as soon as he loses his outline, but if you try to 'pull' him into shape with your hands rather than 'push' him into shape using your legs, then you are likely to keep losing it.

A horse is 'on the bit' when he is working in a good outline, *and* when he is accepting hand and leg without resistance. True impulsion and working on the bit go hand in hand. You won't keep one for long without the other.

Q

Please can you tell me how to improve my transition from trot to canter? I seem to lose my position completely and the horse just goes faster until he breaks into canter, usually on the wrong leg.

A

Aim to keep a steady trot. If your sitting trot is not very good, then only sit down when you feel your horse is really ready to canter. Have a clear idea in your mind of the aid to canter. Ask as you are coming round a corner or a circle. Keep your outside leg back, lean back a little so that you don't bounce, and you should achieve a good strike off.

Preparation is the key to a good transition. If your careful preparation goes wrong, then be patient and start again. Always avoid muddling through – one mistake may lead to another.

Q

I have been told that I ride crookedly. Please could you tell me what this means and if it affects my pony?

A

Your weight should be central in the saddle, and the saddle must be straight on the pony's back. If you ride with one stirrup shorter than the other, or with your body twisted slightly, this makes you unevenly balanced. This means in turn that the pony finds it easier to turn one way or the other, to lead with one particular leg in canter, or to bend to one side rather than the other.

Very few people start riding able to sit absolutely straight. If you are left or right handed, the whole of that side of your body is stronger. Ponies, too, are naturally stronger to one side.

Have a friend check your position from in front and behind. Your spine should seem to 'grow' up in a straight line from the middle of the pony's back. Always check that your stirrups are level, and aim to have an equal feel in each of your seat bones.

Q

Please can you tell me what 'impulsion' is? How do I know if my pony has 'impulsion'?

A

'Impulsion' is quite simply the controlled desire to go forward. If you are having to work hard with your legs all the time, then your pony does not have 'impulsion'. If your pony 'hots up' and takes short rapid steps with his head in the air, then he may have energy, but it is not 'impulsion' because he is not going forward freely, and the energy is not under control.

Q

I can't seem to control my lower legs during schooling sessions. They flap all the time. Could you tell me what might be causing this?

A

You are not sitting deep enough, and as a result are 'fixing' your knees against the saddle. If, at the same time, you are trying to ride with over-long stirrups, you don't have enough weight in your heels to steady your lower legs.

See if you can have a few lunge lessons and work without stirrups to deepen your seat. Aim to have your stirrups feeling just slightly short when you take them back; this makes it much easier to soften your knee and thigh, keeping weight in the heels. Improvement may not be instant but it *does* come gradually.

Developing jumping skills

However thrilled you are with jumping, and no matter how eager you are to move on to the next stage, remember that you must build up experience and skills gradually.

Establishing your position

If you have weekly lessons you may find that the jumping position takes a while to establish. Shorten your stirrups and ride jockey style while trotting or cantering round the arena.

This is an excellent exercise to help your jumping position, providing you maintain your own balance without using the pony's mouth to keep you out of the saddle. It's also a good warm-up exercise before *any* jumping session and is often used by experienced riders, either to get a stuffy horse going or to settle a 'fizzy' one.

Training over low fences

Your instructor is unlikely to make your fences too big at this stage. Bear this in mind if you are practising with a pony at home. Professional show jumpers practise over low fences, concentrating on perfecting their style. Style is much more important than height.

The best exercises are those which promote agility in the horse, developing activity in his quarters and hocks so that they act like coiled springs and push him upward at take-off. Over the fence he should stretch his head and neck forward and down, while rounding his back. This action can be obtained best with gridwork (going down a straight line of fences) and small parallels and not by increasing the jump size.

At this stage, the most important points are correct position and a light contact with the horse's mouth.

▲ **When learning** to jump you have to repeat the same stage several times before you can advance. Trotting over poles is a good way to prepare for a jumping session. Lead the pony over the poles before you start so he knows what to expect.

Practising over trotting poles

► **Early lessons** involving trotting poles, building up to gridwork, are the basis of good jumping. Even when you are more experienced, use trotting-pole exercises as refreshers.

▲ Position the poles about 1m (3ft) apart.

▲ At first walk carefully over the poles.

96

▲ **Trotting** over poles not only gets your pony going, but it also gives you time to check your balance and perfect your jumping position.

▲ Aim toward the middle of the pole.

▲ Check that the pony picks up his feet.

► **Don't underestimate** the importance of gridwork in improving your position and rhythm. Here a rider negotiates a tricky series of low fences with only a bounce between each one. Her position would be better if her legs were further back and her body further forward.

▼ **A good ground line** and wings at the sides make jumps clearly visible and help prevent horses running out. Inviting fences mean your first few attempts at uprights are much easier.

The perfect approach

The way in which you arrive at a fence is probably more important than the jump itself. Trotting poles and gridwork teach you how to make a good approach followed by a straight and steady path over the obstacles.

Look for your line of approach from halfway down the previous long side of the school. When you turn into the approach and are straight, fix your eyes on some point in the distance and ride toward it. The fences will disappear beneath you.

Rhythm and stride

Notice that your instructor varies the distances of the poles and jumps, depending on what the exercise is and also on the length of stride of different ponies. Learn from this and try to build up an idea of what your horse is doing underneath you.

Just as you did when you first learnt the paces, think about the rhythm. Count the beats of the trot in your head '1 – 2, 1 – 2' and check whether they have a regular beat. Every second beat is a complete stride.

This means you can practise counting

the number of strides the pony is taking between the poles. As you get better at this you can begin to tell what the problem is if your pony trips over a pole – whether it's because the distance is too long or too short for him.

Gridwork exercises

There is a variety of grid exercises to practise – starting with cross-poles, you can introduce a pole behind them to make a small spread or just put one of the cross-poles horizontal to make a small upright fence.

Gradually the trotting poles will be removed although the instructor may leave one as a placing pole to help the pony arrive correctly at the first fence. This may be about 2.4-2.7m (8-9ft) – no stride – or 5.4-6m (18-20ft) – one stride – in front of the fence, but the rider should continue to ride for the fence, not for the placing pole. It is *not* advisable to include such a placing pole in a canter exercise.

Eventually you will be popping down a grid, and will be ready to start thinking about combinations and different types of fences put together as a small course.

Coping with problems

Running out is usually caused by the rider. To stop a pony running out, always ride strongly. When approaching an obstacle, aim straight toward the fence and keep your legs against the pony's side to prevent wavering. Presenting the pony at the fence at an angle often encourages him to run out.

Make sure your practice fences are low, wide and inviting with a good ground line and wings to help keep the pony in the centre. Above all, ride positively at all times.

Refusals are often the result of indecisive riding. Ride strongly and give the pony a clear approach so he can see the fence.

However, if a refusal is caused by naughtiness on the pony's part you need to smack him smartly on his hindquarters and ride more firmly next time. You must establish that you are the one who is in charge – not the pony.

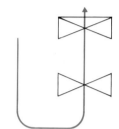

right approach

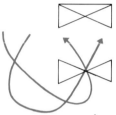

wrong approach

▲ **Turning into a fence** too sharply is often the cause of running out.

▲ **Always ride straight** toward a fence or the horse may run out.

▼ **If the pony senses** that his rider is hesitant, he is likely to refuse.

Water jump: Jumping low fences with a cup of water in your hand is a merciless judge of how steady your balance is!

How much water is left? You can feel justly proud if there's *any* water in the cup after a series of jumps!

How much water is left?

Better jumping know-how

The key to jumping well is to keep working on the basics. Lungeing, bareback riding and jumping with no hands or no stirrups all help to improve your technique and style.

Position and style

When you practise your 'flat' work, think of the jumping course as a dressage test with obstacles. Your ability to push forward and to ride straight and in rhythm is the foundation for successful jumping.

Try to have an instructor there. An extra pair of eyes can be invaluable in pointing out problems and noting any ways in which your style can be improved. This way, you can correct small faults before they become bad habits.

You should also 'feel' what is going on underneath you, so go back on the lunge from time to time. You can concentrate on establishing a good position while your instructor assesses you both.

Remember to sit into the horse and to use your back and seat as well as legs. This helps the pony to bring his hocks underneath him and so propel himself forward both on the flat and over jumps.

At one with the horse

Intersperse general sessions with exercises geared specifically toward jumping improvements.

The closest contact you can have with a horse is to ride without a saddle. Practise riding around the field bareback. It does wonders for your position and your sensitivity.

Try rising to the trot *without* saddle or stirrups. Then just let your legs grow as long as they can. Allow your lower back to absorb the energy coming up from the horse.

Avoid the temptation to grip. Aim to sit in balance with your weight coming down through your seat bones – and you're on the way to that all-important independent seat!

Look – no hands!

Jumping a low grid of fences without stirrups and with your arms folded is an excellent exercise to improve balance and suppleness.

Again, you'll need guidance from someone watching on the ground. When you feel confident, you can go on to an even better test. Try holding a cup of water (without spilling a drop) when

▼ **Lunge practice and bareback riding** both improve your balance and posture. You can safely jump and exercise without holding the reins when the instructor has control of the pony. And by riding without a saddle you can feel every stride and learn to move in harmony with the horse.

Rushing away from a fence or landing out of balance are problems linked with a faulty take off. Be ready to sit up and rebalance your pony as you land, especially if he has 'pecked' (stumbled) on landing as a result of a big jump.

Too often horse and rider land in a heap because the rider is unable to take up the rein and ride forward.

So remember to give the pony plenty of help. Keep him well-balanced into the fence, keep your legs on and try to maintain constant contact with the bit.

▼ **Falling off** happens to every rider, however experienced. Try to roll yourself into a ball before you hit the ground as this lessens the impact. And *always* wear a well-fitting hard hat.

you jump ... then you'll really see how good your balance is!

Remember, much as you may love jumping, to restrict your practice sessions in time (up to 45 minutes), number (twice a week) and height (up to 1m/ about 3ft). Straying from this rule and trying to do too much only makes both horse and rider stale and so creates more rather than less problems.

Parting company

There are bound to be times when you fall off the pony, particularly when jumping. But you can take steps to avoid it. If you ride the same pony regularly, learn to tune into his moods so you know when he is feeling tense and liable to 'shy' at a fence. Aim to be as supple and fit as possible so that your balance is good – lungeing helps a lot.

If you do fall you should, of course, be wearing a hard hat to protect your head. Try to remember to curl into a ball. This lessens the impact and keeps you out of the way of the pony's hoofs.

Pony problems

Most of the pony's faults are man-made – novice horses and novice riders are not a good mix. You can improve your skills by having some lessons on an experienced jumping horse. This teaches you what it feels like to jump correctly. Provided you have the horse straight and balanced on a short, bouncy stride and you are sitting quietly and independently, ready to go with the horse, you can leave it up to him. Presenting the horse correctly is all you need to do.

Problems with the take off

Taking off too early and too far away from the obstacle can be caused by a horse rushing at a fence – because of bad balance or lack of confidence. The horse tends to flatten over the fence, achieving little height. He may dislodge a pole as the hindlegs come down too early.

If rushing becomes a problem, renew the horse's confidence by jumping a grid of smaller fences. Make sure that the horse is straight and balanced, moving steadily and rhythmically.

Taking off too late is a similar problem. The horse 'gets under' the fence and may knock it down with a foreleg.

For both faults, try riding a circle in front of the fence. Incorporate the fence within the circle once the horse settles, so that he learns to find his way accurately to the take-off point. Always rebalance and settle before attempting to jump again.

Jumping out of trot also helps to balance the horse. Be prepared to go back a few stages, using trotting poles to help his footwork. Raise the poles off the ground and trot over them again, with no-stride or one-stride distances between each jump.

Placing poles: To give a horse more confidence and make sure he arrives in the right place for take off and with enough energy, use placing poles. Put a pole about three metres/yards before the fence (the distance varies with the size of the pony and the scope of the fence) so that the last stride before take off is over the pole.

Start with small jumps and gradually make them higher. When you can jump more than 60cm (2ft) with the placing pole, try some single fences without it.

Placing poles

Taking off too early

Taking off too late

Jumping faults

▼ **A common jumping fault** is tipping to one side and looking down at the ground. This means that your weight is unevenly distributed, which unbalances the pony.

It also shows that you're not looking ahead and thinking about the next jump!

For successful jumping you need thorough groundwork, a good position and steady balance – and the confidence that comes from having all three. If your pony is not jumping smoothly and cleanly, it may be your riding that is at fault.

The jumping position

When riding on the flat, you sit up tall and keep a straight line through your shoulder, hip and heel. This is your 'line of balance', which allows you to ride with the least interference of the pony's natural movement.

In jumping, this 'line of balance' has to be altered so that your pony can lift himself and round his back over a fence. You have to adopt a 'forward' seat. Here, your weight is taken over your knee, lower legs and heels so that your seat is light in the saddle.

This is done by shortening the stirrups and folding your upper body forward. If you ride with your stirrups too long, you will find it hard to keep still in this position – your lower legs and upper body swing about.

Behind the movement

Sitting 'behind the movement' is a common fault. This happens if you don't

fold far enough forward from the hips. As the pony takes off, you are left behind and have to hang on to the reins to prevent a fall – known as 'catching the horse in the mouth'.

If you have this problem, try lowering your tummy and chest while still looking ahead between the pony's ears. This makes sure that the whole of your upper body is brought into balance. Sometimes it feels as if you have brought your body forward, when in fact you have only rounded your shoulders.

If a pony gets caught in the mouth too often by a rider who is 'left behind', he may refuse to jump because it is so uncomfortable. The rider presses down on the pony's back just when he needs to round it. This causes his head to lift and his back to hollow, pushing his hindlegs down on the jump.

It is worth spending some time improving your position on the flat and over low fences to correct this fault.

In front of the movement

Getting 'in front of the movement' is less serious for the pony but not safe for you! It comes from a weak leg position with too little weight in your heels. Your lower leg then flies back when the pony is in the air.

Without the support of the lower leg on landing, you fall forward on the pony's withers, and are not ready to ride forward until your balance is regained. More seriously, if your weight is always too far forward, you are almost guaranteed to fall off should the pony suddenly refuse.

He is more likely to refuse, too, because you are not in a good position to drive him forward. A rider with this fault usually has the reins too short and the hands too far up the pony's neck. The best hand position is only a few centimetres in front of the saddle, level with the withers.

▼ **This rider is** sitting down in the saddle, instead of folding forward to take her weight off the horse's back.

Her lower leg is too far forward and her heel is raised, so she is unable to let the weight come down into her legs to make her seat light.

She is having to hang on to the reins to stay with the horse. This is restricting his jump – his head is raised and his back is hollow.

PRACTICE ON THE GROUND

The jumping position can be practised on the ground. Turn your toes out very slightly so that you take your weight on the balls of the feet and heels.

Place your feet far enough apart to allow for the width of a pony. Bend your knees and, keeping your back flat so your spine is straight, fold forward, lowering your shoulders. Your arms are free and you should feel your leg muscles working to hold this position.

An independent seat

With the correct stirrup length and good balance and position you have an 'independent' seat. To achieve this, try *not* to hold on to the mane or a neck strap during practice. If you do, you deceive yourself into thinking that your position is good when in fact it is your hands that are keeping you in place.

With an independent seat you should quickly gain confidence in your ability to stay 'with' your pony over a jump. If you are not confident you will be tense and stiff and tempted to grab for a handful of mane in case of emergency. This restricts your pony and encourages him to jump awkwardly.

If you are unsure of yourself, the pony senses this and loses confidence as well. As a result, he may refuse or jump with

a hollow back, or take off in the wrong place.

Quiet hands

Quiet, still hands go a long way toward getting the best from your pony. You do not have to try and 'lift' him over a fence by raising your hands. The jump comes from the thrust of his hindlegs, not from his head and neck. He needs the freedom of his head and neck to balance.

There is also no need to push your hands right up the pony's neck, as this is more likely to make him bring his head up and so spoil the jump. If you have an independent seat and your hands 'soften' as he takes off, he has all the freedom he needs.

The pony decides where and how he should take off several strides before the

Some common jumping mistakes

Behind the movement

In front of the movement

'Lifting' the horse over the fence

Pushing the hands up the neck

jump. You can help by adjusting his stride in advance. This is done through quiet rein contact and pushing legs.

If you drop the contact at the last moment, however, or give the pony a sudden kick in the ribs, he gets confused and is likely to refuse.

Fiddling with the reins, where you are constantly changing the contact, causes tension and anxiety, often leading to the pony 'hotting up' and throwing his head in the air when asked to jump.

Combined faults

It is important to sit quietly when jumping. If you try to 'do too much' you interfere with the pony's concentration and he loses his fluency.

Other faults can develop from over-vigorous riding. A common problem is flapping elbows. If your elbows stick out each time you jump, your hands fix in to the pony's neck.

Faults often go in groups and flapping elbows tend to combine with standing on your toes and rounding your back. Similarly, tipping to one side goes with looking down instead of straight ahead, and kicking your lower legs back.

In other words, more than one part of your body may be involved, with one fault 'causing' another. It is worth bearing this in mind if you have a particular problem you can't cure however hard you try.

Almost certainly if you go back to checking your leg position and the 'flatness' of your back, and try to sit quietly, the other problems will solve themselves.

STAYING FORWARD

In the early stages, stay in a forward position *between* as well as over fences to make quite sure your position is good.

Later, you will find that you can sit up straighter between jumps and keep your pony more collected. The jumping position will come naturally as the pony takes off. This only comes from experience – if you try it too soon you have to fling yourself forward to catch up with the pony!

Grabbing the mane

Flapping elbows

Dropping the contact

Fiddling with the reins

Your jumping problems solve

Most riders have some bad habits when it comes to jumping. It's important to recognize any faults you have as they often influence the way your pony jumps. Before you blame the pony for not jumping well, check that your own position is correct.

Finding the problem

If you think that there might be something wrong with your jumping – but you are not sure what it is – go and see an instructor. Even if you think that your jumping position is fine, you should have a jumping lesson regularly. Someone watching you can see any problems clearly. Once you know what you're doing wrong you can learn to correct it and so improve your jumping.

▼ You should adopt the correct jumping position whether you're jumping fences or a natural obstacle like water. Always look ahead so you can see where your next fence is and allow the horse to stretch his head and neck by moving your hands forward.

Q

When I jump I tend to be 'left behind' and sometimes I catch my pony in the mouth. How can I prevent this?

A

This is a problem which can be solved by going back to basics. Some ponies seem to take any amount of 'punishment' in their mouths and continue to try, whatever happens. However, this is no way to reward a pony – so it's important to find out wh you're left behind.

Inexperience and lack of confidence
re the usual causes. To cure this habit,
o back to trotting over poles, in
umping position. Push your hands up
he pony's neck so he is working on a
ompletely loose rein. Next tie a knot in
he reins and again trot over the poles
a jumping position. Keep your arms
retched out either side. This exercise
mproves your balance and stops you
urting the pony in the mouth.

Build up the trotting poles into a low
umping grid and practise jumping the
ences calmly – concentrating on riding
a the correct position.

If your pony jumps 'big' this helps him
take his time and place himself better.

Q

I find it hard not to look down when I jump. Can you tell me how I can make myself look ahead?

A

Looking down is a very common fault and it is important to correct it. Any shift in your weight, or your centre of balance over the pony, affects the way that he jumps and lands.

When you ride on the flat, learn to look where you're going. There is no need to look down at your horse – he'll still be there! Keep your head up and look around you from time to time to keep your neck supple and relaxed. Try to *feel* the pony underneath you.

It is exactly the same when you come to jump. Practise riding in jumping position – and keep looking straight out between the horse's ears. Make sure you look for the fence well in advance. Once you approach a fence, fix your eyes on a point in the distance and ride toward that. Remember that when you are riding a course you need to look for the next fence while you're still in the air. You can't do that if you look down.

Q

My lower leg shoots back when I jump. What can I do about it?

A

First check that your stirrups are the correct length for jumping. Riders often try to jump with the stirrups too long and this can cause the lower leg to move back suddenly.

Make sure that your position is correct. If you are perched forward on your 'fork' rather than balanced on your seat bones your lower leg is likely to be thrown back.

The main problem with an incorrect leg position is that you are pushing yourself – and probably your pony – off balance. It could also lead to a fall because you are perched insecurely. Practise cantering in jumping position and turn your toes out slightly. This pushes more weight into the heel and gives you better contact between your lower legs and the horse's sides.

Q

I never know when my pony is going to take off for a jump. Sometimes he takes an extra little step that I don't expect. Have you any advice?

A

Young ponies with inexperienced riders often have this problem. The answer is to return to trotting poles and small grids. Make sure you leave a placing pole in front of the jumps in the grid so that both you and the pony can judge when to take off.

It's best not to interfere with your pony. Just make sure that you are in the correct position. Ride for the fence – not the placing pole – and move your hands forward when he takes off.

Until your pony is more experienced, remain in trot for your approach. This helps him to keep balanced and encourages him to jump well.

Q

Can you describe what instructors call 'the forward seat'? I'm never quite sure what it means.

A

The 'forward seat' is when you are in balance with the horse when he jumps rather than behind the movement with your legs stuck out in front of you. It was developed by Italian cavalry officer Federico Caprilli toward the end of the last century.

To adopt the forward seat, shorten your stirrup leathers by about two holes. This allows you to lean forward. Move your hands forward and let your pony stretch his head and neck. Remember to keep your head up and look forward. In this position you stay over the pony's centre of balance and allow him to jump naturally.

▼ **Most people today** jump in the 'forward seat'. This position is the best for both horse and rider as it allows the horse to jump naturally and the rider to stay in balance with him. An Italian cavalry officer, Federico Caprilli, developed the 'forward seat' around the year 1900.

Rider fitness

![horse icon] **STIRRUP LENGTH**
The length you have your stirrups is extremely important. Always ride at the length you aim to use in competition or hunting, so that your muscles are primed to this position. Never alter the length on the day, because your muscles will be unused to the difference and will ache or, worse, go into cramp.

Riding is a sport, and every sport requires fitness. However, in riding there are added dangers to not being fit enough. An unfit rider tires easily and loses strength, which can make the difference between staying on or falling off. He is also unable to help when his *horse* is a little tired, or in trouble.

The three 'S's

Every individual sport demands its own specific type of fitness, and you use different muscles for different sports. The type of fitness you need for riding, and how fit you need to be, varies according to how strenuous the activity – for example, hacking and show jumping require far less in rider fitness than hunting and eventing.

Strength: Fitness for riding involves muscular strength to a certain extent. This doesn't mean 'brute force' but, rather, the ability to use your muscles to the full, so enabling you to control the pony.

Stamina, which allows you to use the necessary muscles repeatedly and over a long period of time, is of much greater importance for the horse rider. It is achieved by a steady build up of fitness targeted at your particular activity.

Suppleness: As you become fitter, your suppleness improves, meaning you can use your muscles to their utmost. If your muscles are unfit, they ache and go into cramp which makes them stiff. By working the muscles, suppleness improves which in turn prevents stiffness occurring.

Weight and diet

A fit person carries little excess weight. Any visible fat on either a person or a horse indicates that there is an equal number of fatty deposits hidden from sight – around the heart and other internal organs. This puts a strain on these organs when they are asked to work hard.

Every sportsman needs a balanced

HARD GOING
Race riding is the most rigorous of all horse sports for the rider and, strangely enough, flat racing is more taxing than racing over fences. This is because the rider never changes position on the flat while, by moving position over a fence, the muscles have a momentary rest and stretch.

► **Any sporting activity** where competition is involved requires physical effort, and to maintain this effort over a period of time demands fitness. The rider also has a special duty to his horse – it is unfair to expect a horse to perform well if the rider has not prepared himself correctly. Three-day eventing is one of the most gruelling disciplines.

diet with the correct vitamin and mineral intake. However, a rider's diet is probably not as crucial in its content as that of top athletes. In riding, it is the horse who is put to the most severe test. The rider must be fit enough to help his horse, but the same effort is not demanded from him as from his horse.

The best exercise

The only way to develop proper fitness for riding, is to ride. There is no real substitute, because no other activity replaces the effort required to remain in balance and control a moving horse. You can do exercises to stretch and work some of the muscles necessary for riding, but these can't do more than 'tone' them up.

How *much* riding is necessary depends entirely on what the rider and horse combination is aiming to do. Normally it is enough if the rider does all the work involved in preparing for the competition on his horse. By producing a fit horse, the rider is automatically making himself fit as well.

The problem of fitness arises when the rider is otherwise occupied (at work or

school) and someone else is building up the horse or pony's fitness. If you only ride occasionally, you can't expect to become fit enough without taking some other form of exercise.

Alternative exercise

If you are unable to ride every day, or are aiming to ride competitively, it is helpful to take part in some other activity such as jogging, skipping or swimming. Riding in a competition is very hard work and can soon leave you feeling out of breath. Twenty minutes' hard swimming, or 15 minutes of jogging or skipping, a few times a week, can make all the difference.

Other activities such as aerobics can also be of help in a fitness programme, but should be done under the supervision of a qualified teacher to avoid strain. All general stretch and bend exercises help to increase suppleness.

Non-riding exercise is also very useful for maintaining your fitness throughout the year, or if your riding tends to be 'seasonal' to coincide with competitions or hunting. Because slack muscles are more prone to strain and damage, keep-

◄ **Standing up** in the stirrups strengthens your leg and back muscles. Keep your knees bent and let the weight drop down into your heels. Don't try to do too much too soon: build up the length of time slowly.

▼ **Riding without stirrups** is a good exercise to increase your level of fitness. It improves general suppleness and helps to strengthen the leg muscles.

ing up year-round fitness helps avoid problems when you start riding again after a break.

Leg work

There are various exercises which work your 'riding' muscles a little harder, so making them stronger. One way to strengthen your leg and back muscles – as well as improving your balance – is to stand up in the stirrups. It is a good idea to hold on to a neck strap so you don't catch the pony in the mouth if you do lose your balance.

Stand up, then allow all the weight to drop into your heels. Keep your knees bent, and all the while think to yourself 'knees down, heels down'. This exercise stretches your calf muscles and builds up your thighs, as well as working your back muscles. To begin with, do this for a couple of minutes, and gradually build up to 20 minutes.

Another useful exercise is riding without stirrups. This helps suppleness and works the leg muscles very hard. The length of time spent riding without stirrups should be increased gradually – as with any exercise – to prevent muscle strain occurring.

4 Training your pony

Home schooling

To enjoy your riding to the full, you want a pony that is well mannered, supple, forward going and obedient. Some schooling is necessary to achieve this aim and, even with few facilities, there is plenty you can do to improve your pony's all-round performance.

How to begin

When you're starting your schooling programme it's helpful to take advice from a properly qualified riding instructor. A professional can assess your riding and your pony's natural ability and level of training. It's a good idea to return for 'top-up' lessons every month or so, to help you as you progress to more advanced movements.

On the lunge

Lungeing is an excellent way of keeping your pony fit and supple when your time and space are limited. Be aware, however, that it is hard work for a pony and he must already be in fairly fit condition before you start this type of schooling. Also bear in mind the strain on the pony's legs if your lunge circle has become boggy or hard with frost.

◄ **Schooling your pony** improves his balance and makes him more comfortable to ride, whether you want to compete or simply hack in the country.

Keep your lungeing sessions short – not more than about 20 minutes – making sure that you work the *same amount of time* on both reins.

Aim to have the pony working actively from his quarters up into a contact with the side-reins if you are using these. Don't use side-reins to force the pony into an outline – they should never be so short that his face comes behind the vertical. Adjust them so that they are just long enough to encourage him to round his back and seek down for the contact. Keep the side-reins of equal length on each side.

Schooling hacks

All ponies are different and some need more work than others – you must know your own pony. However, don't forget that you can do useful work while out hacking. In the relaxed atmosphere outside the arena you may find the pony more receptive to your commands than when you are struggling in the school.

One essential to remember while trotting is to change your diagonal regularly – riding the same number of strides on each diagonal. Most ponies prefer you to sit on a particular diagonal as they tend to be more supple on one side. It may seem strange at first to use the opposite one, but you must if your pony is to become straight and balanced.

As you trot along the track, decide

DRESSAGE
See pages 134-149 for more information on dressage.

▼ **Your local riding** school may have an all-weather arena that you can use. The surface is specially designed for horses so that you can ride even if the ground is frosty.

which rein you are on (depending on your diagonal) and think about riding your pony forward from your inside leg to your outside hand. Ride him straight, encouraging him to take the contact with the bit and your hand.

Along bridleways or across fields you could try some leg-yielding two or three steps out from the side, ride straight for two or three steps and then leg-yield back to the side again. Do this in walk as well as trot. As you progress, you can use the hedges or fences as the outside track and practise steps in shoulder-in, travers or renvers. This is probably easiest after coming around a corner which serves as your preparatory circle. (*Never* try to do dressage movements on roads.)

If you have to stop on your hacks to open and close gates, take the opportunity to practise a turn about the forehand. Make a change of direction by asking for a quarter or half pirouette to encourage the pony to engage his hocks fully – this helps to keep him supple.

Such schooling sessions can be good fun and much more interesting for you both than confining yourselves to the dressage arena.

These exercises help the pony to become more supple and obedient as well as straightening him and improving his performance. Remember to let him relax, however, and don't spend the entire hack asking him to work.

Transitions

As you walk and trot along, think about the quality of your transitions, remembering that they should all be ridden *forward*. When you canter, ask for a particular lead and don't let the pony simply strike off on his favourite.

A few good canter paces followed by trot and walk and then more upward transitions make a stiff pony supple.

If frequent changes of pace excite him, you may need to work him a little more beforehand, or give the pony a good canter to settle him. The same goes in the school; if your pony is not in the frame of mind for work or is bursting out of his skin you can wake him up or settle him down by cantering in the forward seat until he's beginning to blow a bit.

Knowing what your pony needs is important here, as is taking professional advice from someone who can see you both working together. All riders, at whatever level, need a pair of eyes on the ground.

Warming up

The ideal schooling ground is an all-weather arena of 20 × 40m (66 × 132ft), with dressage markers. Riding schools usually have these facilities, so see if your local school rents its arena for winter use when conditions can be difficult at home.

If you are aiming at competition work, schooling hacks won't be enough and

▼ **Lungeing Australian style:** This method can be used if a pony is fresh at a show and no headcollar or cavesson is available. However, Australian style lungeing is not recommended as it pulls the bit through the mouth. If lungeing to the bit, it is better to slip the rein through the inside ring and attach to the outside ring.

you need to do more formal work.

Always remember to warm up your pony thoroughly before starting concentrated work. He is just like an athlete or gymnast who has to limber up so that his muscles are working at maximum efficiency.

Take a gradual contact through a series of large turns and circles. Make sure that you ride through each corner as though it is part of a circle. Use the inside leg to make him take a contact on the outside rein. As he begins to settle, you can take up the contact and go through your work programme. Practising the movements from a preliminary or novice dressage test is fun and gives you a helpful structure to work around.

It's just as important to allow your pony to cool down after a schooling session. Let him take the rein and stretch down his head and neck while trotting and walking large circles. If he stretches readily then you know he's worked hard!

Be critical of yourself and learn to 'feel' when the pony is going well or badly. If something doesn't seem to be working, leave it for a while and return to a simple exercise which you and your pony do well – be flexible in your approach. The time to finish a session is when schooling is going well – you should never end on a bad note. Remember that *you* may be the reason for a bad day, not your pony!

▲ **When you ride** on the roads, you must put traffic awareness first and concentrate on schooling only when you are on bridleways or in open country. If you trot, change diagonals frequently to prevent your pony becoming stiff on one side.

◄ **Opening gates from** horseback provides the opportunity to practise school movements such as turn on the forehand and rein back. It's also much less trouble for the rider than dismounting!

How to lunge a pony

Lungeing has been used in training horses and ponies for hundreds of years. It has many benefits for the pony and you don't have to be a brilliant rider to be good at lungeing.

What does lungeing do?

The great advantage lungeing has over riding is that the pony can learn to go well without the hindrance of carrying someone. The rider's weight can upset his balance or put extra strain on muscles doing new and unaccustomed work.

Lungeing also makes the pony more supple and, with side-reins, gets him working in a correct outline. An over-excited, cold or stiff pony often gives a much easier ride if he is lunged for ten minutes first.

From your point of view, you can still work and exercise the pony even if he can't be ridden – perhaps because his saddle needs mending or the pony has a sore back. It is also helpful to watch your own pony working and to teach him obedience to voice commands.

Even if you know you couldn't possibly train your pony to high-school dressage level, it is still worth learning

▼ **The lunge whip:** There is a special way to hold the whip when not in use. Wind the lash round the length of the handle and tie it in a knot at the base. This stops it trailing on the ground.

You'll manage it more quickly if an expert shows you the first time.

► **When leading the pony,** tuck the whip under your arm and hold it out behind you so it doesn't catch the pony's legs. Practise at home *without* a pony until you get the hang of it.

how to lunge. Any calm, sensible and practical person can learn quite quickly, although a certain amount of know-how and horse sense helps. Always learn with a trained pony, watch experienced people lungeing and get a sound knowledge of the basics before you start on a novice horse.

Keep the sessions short – up to 30 minutes in total with a very fit pony. Lungeing can be done every day but once or twice a week is adequate.

What you need

Find somewhere safe to lunge before buying a lot of expensive equipment. For a pony, a square 15m (50ft) wide is enough. This could be a flat area in the corner of a field or one end of a schooling area. Remember that the centre, where you stand, must be as flat as the edge of the lungeing circle. It is easier to judge the size and shape of the circle if you mark out a square with poles or cones. Poles should be wedged so they can't roll about.

The only other equipment you need at first is a lungeing rein and a whip. The less expensive whips are usually light and easy to handle. A lungeing cavesson

HOLDING THE LUNGE-REIN

Hold the rein in the hand nearest the horse's head. Coil it up with your thumb on the topmost loop. Let it out slowly by lifting your thumb and dropping a coil at a time.

Practise coiling it on to your hand and letting it out smoothly. It's easiest if someone helps you: a friend can take the pony's place and hold the other end of the rein!

VOICE CONTROL

Good voice control is essential. Keep your tone varied – bright and quick to encourage upward transitions, low and soothing to slow down.

Don't attempt cantering until you are fully in control in walk and trot and can get quick responses to your voice commands without using too much whip.

▲ Extra tack: The pony may be wearing a saddle, either so you can attach side-reins, or because you intend to ride after the lunge session. The stirrup irons must be securely run up the leathers so they don't rub the saddle or slip down.

Side-reins teach the pony to accept the rein contact but needn't be used when you are first learning how to lunge.

is best for attaching the lunge-rein but, if you don't have one, use a headcollar. Wearing gloves stops you getting rope burns if the pony pulls away.

The rein and whip

Your aim now is to have your pony working round you with even rein contact and in a perfect circle which touches the four sides of your marked square. You should be able to stand in the middle giving quiet commands to walk, trot, canter or halt without the pony cutting in on the circle. He should be active, attentive and obedient. But the first problem is how to handle the length of the lunge-rein and whip!

To work on the left rein, hold the whip in your right hand. The lunge-rein goes from your left hand to the cavesson (or headcollar if this is all you have at the moment). Coil the lunge-rein carefully so that it doesn't tangle as you let it out. It may help at first to hold the spare end in your right hand and let the rein run through your left hand. This stops you dropping too much rein and tangling it in the pony's legs.

Starting and walking

Start in the middle of the circle, standing next to the pony's girth. With the

Starting off on the left rein

1 Stand in the centre of the circle, with the rein in your left hand and whip in your right. Ask the pony to walk forward.

rein in your left hand, ask him to walk forward (take a few steps yourself if necessary) and quietly bring the whip toward his hindlegs. As the pony goes forward, stay put and let him move away from you, gradually letting out the lunge-rein. Keep repeating the command 'Walk on!' until the pony is walking round the circle and you can take your place in the centre.

Position yourself opposite the girth so

Changing the rein

1 Halt the pony. Tuck the whip under your arm so that it is pointing behind you. Go to the pony's head, winding up the rein as you go to stop it trailing on the ground.

2 Make much of the pony and reward him if he has worked well. Walk round to his off side. He should remain in halt until you tell him to move.

2 As he moves off, stand still. Let out the lunge-rein slowly while he walks forward. Repeat the 'walk on!' command if need be.

3 The pony should walk all round the circle with you in the middle. You should be the point of a triangle with the three sides formed by the pony, rein and whip (inset).

that you are the point of a triangle. The three sides are the pony, the lunge-rein and the lunge whip. Keep turning to face the pony and stand up straight with your elbows bent and close to your sides. Try to relax. Move the whip quietly to keep the pony active and encourage him forward with your left hand on the rein.

Walk to trot

To go from walk to trot, call the pony to attention by saying his name followed by 'Ter-rot!' and a slight raising of the lunge whip. If necessary give the lash a flick (not to hit him or he may charge off at a gallop!). If he is idle, crack the whip but practise this without the pony first.

After a few circuits in trot ask him for walk: 'Waaa-alk'. At the same time, lower the whip but keep it pointing toward the pony. Ask him to halt in the same way, staying out on the circle. Now you are ready to change rein and repeat the exercise on the right rein.

SLOWING DOWN
This can be the hardest part. Don't pull the pony round in a small circle as you may strain his legs.

Put an extra coil in the rein, go toward the pony's head and give a quick jerk on the rein. Repeat your command and reward improvement.

3 Put the lunge-rein in your right hand, and your whip in the left hand, passing it behind your back. You may find it rather cumbersome to manage at first.

4 It is important to work equally on each rein, otherwise you are both likely to become 'one-sided', so repeat the lesson as for the left rein.

Training a pony to jump

The first few weeks of training a pony to jump are the most important in his jumping career. If things go wrong now and he gets hurt, frightened or confused, he will find it very difficult to jump with confidence later on in life.

The trainer

For this reason, you should let somebody experienced take your pony through the basic stages, unless you are already competent.

It is vital that the rider remains in good balance, without interfering either with the pony's mouth or his back, even if he gives a very awkward jump. The pony must feel that he will keep out of trouble, so long as he does his best – although he may make mistakes despite being in capable hands.

Each pony is different and must be brought on at the speed which suits him best. Rush him and he may start refusing. A good pony could then be branded as a 'stopper', when all he needed was a little more time to learn. If possible, work with your trainer. You can help by mov-

ing poles and altering distances and heights. This way you learn how to position the jumps correctly when you take over the ride. You also get to know what your pony's strengths and weaknesses are so you can get the best out of him yourself.

Starting off

Jumping lessons can start when the pony is four years old. Walk, trot and canter should be well established so that he is neither rushing or refusing to go forward freely.

The equipment you need at this stage is very basic: three poles (more if you can get them) and something to raise the poles off the ground by several centimetres. Plastic Bloks are ideal; milk crates, small oil drums or rubber tyres make good

substitutes. You don't need to paint everything in bright colours, although this is helpful when you are preparing for your first competition.

The first phase is often better done on the lunge. Without the interference of a weight on his back, the pony moves more freely. He only needs a lunge cavesson and rein and protective boots.

First lessons

Begin by walking the pony over a single pole on the ground until he is completely confident and relaxed. If he refuses, lead him over or let him follow another pony but do not have a battle or he will associate poles with fighting!

Go on to place two and then three poles in the lunge circle, so that he steps over them each time he goes round. The distance between the poles should give him room to take a few steps in between. Don't worry about precise distance: just leave enough room for the pony to work out for himself how to adjust his stride as he meets the poles.

Give him every chance and don't place two poles very close together. If you do, the pony will probably try to jump them in one go and this won't help him to think about his stride pattern without guidance from his rider.

If the pony lowers his head to look at the poles this is good. He is already learning to round his back properly. But if he rushes and gets over-excited, move so the pole or poles are outside the lunge circle. Once he is walking calmly on the lunge again, move the circle to take him over the poles.

Trotting

You may need to do several lessons in the walk – lasting not more than 15 minutes three or four times a week. Once the pony understands that he must pick his feet up to clear the poles, the trot phase should create few problems.

Lunge him in the same way, with one pole at first until he keeps to a steady trot rhythm. From one pole, go to three, carefully placed trotting poles. The distance between them varies from pony to pony but should match his natural stride. This makes trotting poles easy for him and builds his confidence. Get him used to approaching straight, calmly and with impulsion; working on the lunge encourages a round outline.

Go from three to four or even five

! GROWING PAINS

Until he is at least five years old, the pony should not be asked to jump any great height. He may still have some growing to do and the concussion on landing may damage his joints. For the same reason, avoid any jumping on hard ground.

LUNGE EQUIPMENT

Always use boots as protection against a rap from a pole and in case the pony strikes himself with the opposite foot during jump training. Don't use side-reins when jumping on the lunge – they restrict his movement.

STAGE FRIGHT

If at any time during training a problem develops, go back a stage to confirm the work and avoid confusion.

Good flatwork is the major contribution toward producing good jumping. Improving the flatwork may well correct any slight jumping problems.

★ VARYING THE JUMP

Whether you are working your pony on the lunge or mounted, vary the jump in simple stages. Go from a cross-pole to a straight pole with a ground line and then to a low parallel.

Always increase the width before the height as this encourages good 'bascule' – the rounded outline over a fence.

poles in a line and work from both reins. You may need to wedge the poles so they can't roll and get under the pony's feet.

The first jump

You can place the first jump on its own or at the end of a line of trotting poles. Using the poles first is ideal if you have enough equipment. Put the last two poles together to make a low cross-pole. The line should consist of three trotting poles, a 'missing' pole, followed by the cross-pole itself.

As the pony is already used to approaching a line of poles in a good trot, he will then learn to jump without rushing or losing impulsion. Don't be

► **Walking over one pole** is the first stage in training. Only go on to more poles when the horse is relaxed and takes one in his stride.

surprised if he knocks the jump down the first time – this is a new experience for him and he must learn to pick himself up.

If you are not using trotting poles in front of the jump, make sure the pony is going calmly when you put him at the cross-pole for the first time. Don't move your lunge circle to include the jump until he is working correctly. Always remember to work on both reins during each session.

One pole in front of the fence is always helpful in placing the pony for a correct take off, particularly as you start to vary the look of the fence. This is not a ground line but a placing pole and lies between 1.8–2.7m (6–9ft) in front of the fence. The pony should take off between the pole and the jump. The distance will need altering as the pony gains in confidence and strength.

▲ **Work up to trot** after several lessons in walk. The poles should be about 120cm (4ft) apart, matching the horse's natural stride. Remember to work from both reins, and don't let the horse rush.

► **You can help** the pony's trainer by moving poles, and can learn a lot yourself just by watching an expert at work. The last two trotting poles are pushed together to form a low cross-pole. It's a good sign if the horse is curious and takes a long look at this new obstacle!

► **The first jump:** If you have built up the horse's training stage by stage, he should enjoy popping over his first proper jump. The line of trotting poles leading up to the low fence helps him to approach in a lively trot.

All except one trotting pole can soon be discarded – although you should still use trotting poles at least once a week as a muscle-building exercise and to maintain good habits.

▼ **Mounted jumping:** Start jumping mounted when the pony is obviously confident in the work he is doing. The rider should sit quietly, only doing enough to encourage a correct approach. Too much interference spoils the pony's concentration. It doesn't matter if he canters the last stride before jumping, as long as he doesn't rush off afterwards. Always warm up on the flat for 10–15 minutes before attempting a jump (inset).

Warm up on the flat first

Improving a pony's jumping

If a pony jumps badly, the reason lies somewhere in his past. It may be that he was poorly trained in the beginning or has since been ridden by an unsympathetic rider. Whatever has happened – and it may be impossible to find out the exact cause – it is up to the trainer to correct the faults one by one. In this way, confidence can be restored, and good habits and obedience established.

▼ ► **Most ponies** jump well naturally. They take off at the right point, clear the jump, land smoothly and follow through as fluidly as they approached. Once a rider confuses the pony, however, he may develop faults.

Obedience and sympathy

A pony can only jump well if he goes correctly on the flat. He doesn't need to be highly trained but there are two basics that often need sorting out.

First, obedience to the leg. This doesn't mean simply going forward to a leg aid but also accepting the *feel* of the legs. A pony which shoots forward as soon as he feels the rider's leg against his side can be a real nuisance and very difficult to place correctly at a jump. The same applies to the pony which insists on going sideways at the sight of a jump in spite of the rider's efforts to straighten him out with the leg aids.

Second, the pony should have a good mouth. If he is frightened of the bit, a touch on the reins sends his head up and hollows his back. On the other hand, a pony with 'no mouth' pulls and leans on the rider's hands. Make sure the pony is happy with his bit and obedient to it, and be prepared to change it.

The pony's mouth should improve as he learns to accept the leg. The rider must try to work with a light, consistent contact on the mouth and avoid pulling back when the pony pulls. Most ponies do not settle unless there is a contact as, until then, they worry about where the contact is and when there is going to be a sudden pull on the mouth.

With these two 'basics' sorted out, the pony should be working actively forward, straight and attentive to his rider. He approaches his jumps with confidence, but no rushing!

What can go wrong?

Sadly, most ponies jump less than perfectly. Refusing or running out are the most common problems. Every time this happens, ask yourself why and what can be done to correct the problem. It is worth making a mental list of all possible excuses before deciding that the

▲ A good jump
should be smooth, the pony able to round his back, extend his head and neck, and tuck his feet up neatly while he is in the air.

The follow through needs to be as smooth as the approach if the pony is to be able to tackle the next fence equally well.

pony is just plain naughty. Even if he is, he probably had a very good reason when he started the habit!

Running out is due to lack of straightness in the approach, usually combined with rushing. Sometimes this happens because the pony is frightened of the jump and would rather take an easy way round.

If the fear is not deep-rooted, tackling very low fences and concentrating on a direct, calm approach, sorts out the problem. But a very frightened pony either refuses or takes a huge leap even when he is kept straight.

Fear and bravery

Fear has many causes. It could be that the pony has been pulled in the mouth or has rapped his legs on a pole or perhaps even fallen in the past. It may be that he is over-faced and doesn't know how to jump. If this is the case, it is better to put the jump right down,

Rushing is due to lack of obedience to the rider's aids. The pony's back hollows and his head may go up because he is scared of the feel of the bit.

Rapping a fence is usually because of a bad approach and jumping style. The pony may be over-confident and careless when taking off.

Refusing has a number of causes. The pony may lack agility, be bored with jumping, feel nervous himself or sense his rider's hesitation.

even to ground level, and to build up slowly. Going too high too soon can be off-putting, resulting in the pony not wanting to try at all.

Some ponies are brave and clever and jump even if asked to take off at the wrong place. Others need to have their striding exactly right. These ponies are usually less agile or powerful and need sympathetic riding to get the best from their limited abilities. Ponies usually know their own limitations and have no desire to hurt themselves. If they know they are 'wrong', they refuse.

Boredom and nerves

Boredom and over-jumping can cause refusals. If a pony has been jumping well and, for no apparent reason, gives up, then he may just need a few weeks or even months free of jumping to restore his enthusiasm.

Over-jumping, especially on hard ground, can lead to foot and leg problems so that the pony starts refusing. Such a pony often takes off very close to his fences, using minimum effort so that he can land more softly on the ground. He refuses only the bigger, wider jumps at first and gets progressively worse if forced to continue.

Refusing may come about with a nervous pony if he is put to a type of fence he has never seen before. Careful training at home, using some imagin-ation in fence-building, gradually over-comes this problem, as does intelligent and confident riding.

A rider who expects a refusal or feels over-faced can cause a stop. Doubt is easily put across to a pony so he cannot be blamed for not wanting to jump! This particular fault can be spotted if the pony seems to 'fade' on the approach rather than stop suddenly.

Confidence and care

Although it is important for a pony to be confident over poles, he must also show them respect. Over-confidence can be followed by carelessness and knocking poles down. This is a difficult fault to cure leading to some trainers using rather nasty methods to make the pony pick up his feet properly.

If a pony has been hurt in this way, he may decide that enough is enough and won't jump at all. He may look angry – not frightened – with ears back and tail swishing. Sometimes jumping across country rather than in the ring gets him going again.

Knock-downs are more often caused by a bad approach and/or poor style over the fence. Jumping with a hollow back or a restricted head and neck means the pony has to jump higher to clear the fence. The answer is to re-learn technique: improve his flatwork, get his confidence over low fences and use gridwork.

JUMPING IN STYLE
A good pony does plenty of thinking for himself. Over the smaller fences it is best to let him develop this ability and allow him to find the best place to take off. It is only when the fences get bigger that the rider can try to see and ride for the correct take off point – about the height of the hump plus half that distance again.

! PUNISHING BEHAVIOUR
It is hardly ever necessary to punish for bad jumping. Find out the cause of the problem first. Only if you are 100% sure that the fault cannot be schooled out, should you think of using the whip for anything more than sharpening the pony to your leg.

◄ **Reward** for a good effort is much the best way of ensuring improved jumping habits.

Practising the halt

Introduction to dressage

The word dressage simply means training a riding horse. Any pony can be taught obedience and balanced movement if you ride it thoughtfully and carefully – which is what dressage is all about.

The aims of dressage

The object of training the riding horse is the same as for any athlete or dancer. Exercise and weight training in the gymnasium do for the long-distance runner what dressage does for the horse – they make him strong, supple and agile, and improve his co-ordination.

All well-schooled horses go through a period of dressage training. It is essential for success and enjoyment in all kinds of riding – jumping, gymkhanas, polo, cross country and hacking. By teaching your pony properly you'll help him to stay sound and healthy, gallop faster, turn more quickly, jump higher, be safer and more obedient.

It is a rewarding challenge to train a horse well. But first you need to know a little about the horse's movement in his natural state. Only then can you perfect his paces despite the weight of a rider.

First steps in dressage

The horse is a naturally graceful and swift animal. But when you sit on his back to ride him, you upset his balance and limit the range of his natural paces.

To reduce or, preferably, remove any discomfort – some horses' feet and legs suffer; others get back pain from the rider's weight – you must sit correctly, giving the horse an evenly balanced load to carry. This is one of the reasons why riding instructors pay so much attention to your position in the saddle.

Once you've established a good seat you can aim to improve your pony's natural paces and outline while carrying a rider. Training a horse to perform the walk, trot and canter well is the basis for all dressage training.

Practising your paces

At any pace, your pony should move forward energetically and willingly with a good rhythm. He should be relaxed and looking ahead at all times. Unless going in a straight line, he should be flexed a little to the direction in which he is going. He must be calm and put up no resistance, and be alert to your instructions.

You need to practise the three main paces – walk, trot and canter – until your pony maintains both his balance and rhythm at any speed – and until you do, too! All transitions, particularly trot to canter and back again, should be smooth, calm and quiet.

Study closely how the horse moves. Think about what he is actually doing. Riding becomes really fascinating when

◄ **Practising the square halt** is one of the first steps in training a pony in dressage. A horse should stand still on all four legs with his weight evenly distributed. Always keep contact with your pony's mouth so that he is alert to your instructions.

◄ **Jennie Loriston-Clarke** on Dutch Bid, a chestnut gelding, demonstrates the square halt.

A dressage arena

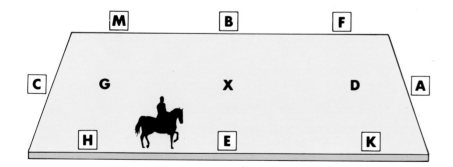

A basic dressage arena measures 20 metres (66ft) wide and 40 metres (132ft) long. Letters are used as markers around the edge and across the middle of the arena. These are traditional and act as points of reference. They have no special meaning.

In a dressage test you and your pony have to perform particular movements that start and finish at a given letter. The examiners test your ability to ask the pony to perform various steps.

They also test your pony's understanding and obedience.

To get used to a dressage arena, start by practising smooth transitions from walk to trot and trot to canter as you reach your chosen letter.

This arena is used for most pony tests, but the international arena (60 metres/198ft) is longer and has more letters. It's used for all international tests and some national ones.

★ **LEARNING THE LETTERS**
One of the easiest ways of remembering the position of the letters round a dressage arena is by learning a rhyme.

Try to memorize a phrase like All King Edward's Horses Carry Many Brave Fighters.

The first letter of each word indicates a letter in the dressage arena. This way you'll know the letters off-by-heart in no time at all.

★ **DRESSAGE TESTS**

There are several grades of dressage tests. The simplest give you an opportunity to show how well-established your pony's paces are, and how accurately he makes the transition from one to another.

At the more advanced levels, you have to show your pony's obedience by asking him to step backward. In some tests you have to show how balanced and responsive your pony is by lengthening and shortening the steps at walk, trot and canter, or to show that he can step forward and sideways at the same time.

you understand your pony's stride pattern and you know how to influence this. Each pace has a different action and alters the appearance of the horse.

The walk is a four-time movement in which the horse has three hooves on the ground at any one time. But there's more to it than that. The head and neck swing up and down in rhythm with the stride. To show that he is relaxed and supple your pony's tail should swing softly. The walk must be purposeful. Ideally, your pony looks as though he is off to keep an important appointment: he is not in a hurry and has plenty of time, but he is making sure that he won't be late.

The trot: It is easy to feel, when rising at the trot, that your pony trots in two-time. He should spring lightly along, jumping from one diagonal pair of feet to the other, with a moment of suspension in between when none of his feet are on the ground.

The canter should be a light, swinging pace in which the horse uses his whole body in a soft, relaxed way, nodding his head and neck in rhythm with the stride.

It is a three-time movement – either hindleg lifts and is followed by the other hindleg with its diagonal foreleg and finally the other foreleg. This foreleg is known as the leading leg. If you are cantering to the right, this remaining foreleg should be the right one. If you are cantering to the left, the left foreleg must lead.

The walk

► In dressage, each pace can be executed in various forms including medium, collected, extended and free.

Medium paces are rhythmical and energetic with medium-length strides. In *collected* movements, the horse takes short, elastic steps while in the *extended* version he should reach out and cover as much ground as possible. Finally, *free* paces are on a loose rein, with the horse relaxed but attentive. Start off by practising a medium walk.

▼ Warming up before a competition, French international rider Philippe Limousin practises a medium walk.

The trot

▲ Whether you choose to do a rising or sitting trot (as here) — and whatever variation you're practising — your horse should take regular strides forward,

changing evenly from one pair of diagonal legs to the other. His energy should come from his hindquarters, propelling him forward.

▼ This horse is trotting well but lacks engagement of the hind legs. It would be improved if the hind legs stepped further under the body.

The canter

► Once you and your pony are moving in harmony at the walk and trot, you can concentrate on the canter. In this three-time movement your pony should glide forward energetically.

Make sure you are sitting upright in the centre of the saddle with your weight evenly distributed. This gives a pony complete freedom of movement.

The hindlegs must produce enough force to give a good rhythmical pace. The leading hindleg should tuck forward under the horse.

Dressage: the aids

Dressage is the basis for whatever else you want to do with a horse. It teaches you to give, and the horse to receive, a range of subtle instructions and messages.

Communicating

Communication between horse and rider is one of the most important aspects of dressage training. You have to ask the horse to perform any action simply by using signals.

Squeezing with either or both legs, feeling the reins, or pushing with the seat are your only signals when asking the horse to make a huge number of movements. These range from halt and walk to turning and circling – right up to the advanced dressage movements of piaffe and passage.

In dressage your aim is to *perfect* your aids. The means by which you transmit your instructions remain the same, but your interpretation and transmission of them must improve and become more precise.

◄ **Tutu Sohlberg** warming up on her German-bred horse, Pakistan.

Checking the basics

You and your horse are building on the basis of what you have already learnt. So before moving on to anything new, check your position and run through the aids to make sure you haven't slipped into bad habits.

Your seat should be correct: well-balanced, but relaxed. Your body weight must be supported evenly on the two seat bones. As your aids become more subtle, your horse will assume that a momentary stiffening of your back is an instruction and act accordingly. So you must be balanced perfectly and not wriggle about, because it could be misinterpreted.

Riding is done mainly with the legs: they apply most of the aids and create energy in the horse. You must be correctly placed to close the legs inward, encouraging the horse forward.

The stirrup leathers should hang vertically and the *ball* of your feet should sit on the stirrup irons. This is the best position for applying the leg aid. The legs must not wobble around, otherwise the horse may be confused as to whether or not he is receiving an aid. And the upper half of your leg should stay ➤

★ **LEFT AND RIGHT REIN**
In dressage riding the horse is said to be on the left or the right rein, even when he is going straight ahead. This is because eventually, at the end of the straight line, he will turn left or right.

So when a 'change of rein' is mentioned, this simply means a change of direction.

Using signals

As you progress with dressage, your aids need to become more precise so that the horse understands exactly what you want him to do. You can also use artificial aids when you practise to back up your natural aids. These sharpen the horse's reaction to your instructions.

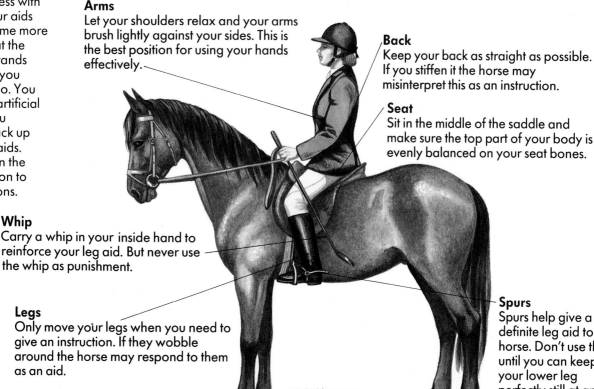

Arms
Let your shoulders relax and your arms brush lightly against your sides. This is the best position for using your hands effectively.

Back
Keep your back as straight as possible. If you stiffen it the horse may misinterpret this as an instruction.

Seat
Sit in the middle of the saddle and make sure the top part of your body is evenly balanced on your seat bones.

Whip
Carry a whip in your inside hand to reinforce your leg aid. But never use the whip as punishment.

Legs
Only move your legs when you need to give an instruction. If they wobble around the horse may respond to them as an aid.

Spurs
Spurs help give a definite leg aid to the horse. Don't use them until you can keep your lower leg perfectly still at any pace.

![horse icon] **'BETWEEN LEG AND HAND'**

Between the leg and the hand is a term often used in dressage. It means that the horse is alert and ready to respond to any command. Energy has been created by the legs and seat, but is being controlled by the hands. This is the ideal position for horse and rider to be in.

absolutely still at all times in dressage.

Sit upright with your shoulders relaxed and let the top part of your arm fall softly against your body. The inside of your sleeve should brush against the side of your jacket. Your elbow should be soft and supple, allowing the horse to adjust the height of his head and the length of his neck with equal ease.

The voice is a useful aid for practice sessions. When you are training you use it to help the horse understand what you are asking him to do. However, in a dressage test you are not allowed to use your voice and you are penalized if you do. You are being tested on the *unspoken* communication between you and your horse.

Artificial aids

The artificial aids are the whip and the spur. These are used as a back-up for the natural aids. In some junior competitions a whip is not allowed, but you may use spurs.

In dressage training, you can carry a long schooling whip to reinforce the leg aid. Dressage whips are longer and narrower than all-purpose whips. This makes them flexible so that you can lightly flick the horse without taking your hands off the reins.

The whip should not be used as punishment. It helps to sharpen your horse's reaction to your leg aid and reduces the need to kick.

The whip should be carried in the inside hand because the inside leg aids are the most important. They are, therefore, the aids which need to be reinforced. You must remember to change the whip to your other hand when you cross the arena.

Spurs are used when a more definite leg aid is required and more energy from the hindquarters is needed. You should only begin to use spurs when you can maintain an independent leg position. If you can't keep your lower leg still, you may hurt the horse.

The advantage of spurs is their precision: you can apply pressure on an exact spot, while your boot heel gives a rather 'woolly' aid.

► **The aim** of a dressage test is to show off the results of all your hard work at home. So a whip is valuable for schooling sessions but need not be used in the ring.

Practising the half halt

The half halt, when a rider asks a horse for a halt but then allows him to go forward, checks a horse's speed at any pace and helps make his strides more springy.

To make a half halt, rest the legs on the horse's sides and restrain the forward movement by giving and taking with the reins. Just as he is about to change the pace ease the reins slightly while keeping the legs firmly on his sides. Asking a horse to slow down and then allowing him to continue helps rebalance him.

Circling

The circle is one of the most basic school movements and it is a good exercise to start practising. It takes some time to make the circle geometrically exact, so don't expect too much from your first attempts. Work on large circles – about 24 metres (26 yards) around – to begin with. The smaller the circle, the more difficult the movement becomes.

To achieve an exact circle, you must give precise instructions. Your horse should be bent slightly round the edge of the circle. On a clockwise circle he should curve a little round your right leg. You ask him to bend to the inside with the fingers of your inside hand, but it is vital to keep a steady contact with your outside hand. Never pull back on the reins.

The touch of your inside leg encourages the horse to go steadily forward, while your outside leg is ready to control the hindquarters if they swing out.

◄ **The circle** is a basic dressage movement that takes time to perfect. Here a rider is put through her paces in the junior classes at Goodwood (the famous English dressage showground).

▼ **Start your practice circles** with turns on a corner. Concentrate on giving precise signals with your hands and legs to control the horse's movements.

Dressage: the paces

The well-trained horse can vary his stride in each pace: he takes longer or shorter steps when asked to do so by his rider.

Variations of pace

Variations in the length of step are known as working, collected, medium and extended paces.

Working paces are generally those natural to the horse before he has had much training. He should be obedient, relaxed and balanced, and move with plenty of energy.

Collected paces: The three big joints of the hindlegs – the hip, stifle and hock – are more flexed and the horse's legs tuck well underneath his body at each step. The horse moves with a shorter, rounder action than in the working paces. The croup is lowered, making the forehand light. The neck is raised and arched and the front of the face is almost vertical.

Medium paces: The horse takes steps which are longer than those of a working pace, but not to the fullest possible extent. He must go with great energy, stretching his head and neck forward a little so he can take longer steps with the forelegs as well as the hindlegs.

Extended paces: The horse strides along with maximum energy, taking steps of the greatest possible length.

The walk

The term 'working walk' is not used: because the horse does not have much scope to lengthen or shorten his walk strides, he could not manage four variations of this gait. The horse works most naturally at 'medium walk'; from there the rider can ask him to work at 'free walk on a long rein'.

This means the rider lets the reins out far enough to allow the horse to stretch his head and neck forward and down. He continues to walk with long, deliberate, generous steps.

Giving the aids

To make your pony shorten or lengthen his steps takes lots of practice and patience, and you will certainly need help from your instructor. The first step is to establish good working paces. You can then ask your pony to take a few lengthened steps, making sure he maintains his balance.

This can be done from either working

◄ **This pair are** going through their paces in a junior dressage competition at Goodwood. Here they are performing the collected trot.

★ **TEMPO**
The 'tempo' of the horse's work (the speed of the rhythm) should stay the same in collected, working, medium or extended paces.

When the horse takes medium or extended steps, he is not increasing the number of steps by running. He goes faster because the steps are longer, not quicker.

▲ **Dressage tack:** For the experienced horse and rider, a double bridle helps in giving precise aids. The dressage saddle is specially designed to help the rider sit upright. It has a deep seat to keep you central in the saddle, and a straighter cut because of the longer leg position.

trot or canter. Make a half halt to balance your pony and get his full attention. Then apply both legs to encourage him to take longer, more powerful steps with the hindlegs. At the same time, let him stretch his head and neck forward a little, while keeping the rein contact.

He should lengthen his outline and take longer steps with his forelegs to match those of his hindlegs. He must keep a clear rhythm, taking steps of equal length. Your instructor will be able to tell you if you've succeeded. When your pony does achieve the lengthening you've asked for, make sure you give him plenty of praise.

At the end of the lengthened steps, it is important to make a smooth transition back to the working pace. Sit up, apply both legs and resist slightly with your hands. As soon as he shortens his steps back to the working pace, relax your hands but keep your legs against him and ride forward. Otherwise he will lose his impulsion and slow down.

Impulsion and collection

Impulsion is the power that the horse creates with his hindlegs. It must not be confused with speed. It is controlled energy produced in the horse by the use of your legs and seat. This energy is received in your hands where it is lightly guided and controlled.

You need impulsion to obtain collection. The object of collection is to 'coil up the spring' of energy in the hindquarters. Once the spring is uncoiled, the energy is released and the horse goes into longer steps.

To collect your pony, he must be submissive and not opposing you. The muscles of his neck and jaw should be relaxed. You cannot try to *force* collection by resisting with your hands.

By using your legs, you ask him for more action from the three major joints of the hindlegs. When the pony uses these joints more he steps further underneath himself with his hindlegs. This causes the croup to lower, which in turn raises the forehand. When this happens, you have obtained a degree of collection.

Once the pony is collected you can ask for medium and eventually extended paces. To do this, you maintain or increase the energy with your legs and let the pony go forward from your hands.

The walk

Working paces

Free walk on a long rein

Collected paces

Collected walk

Medium paces

Medium walk

Extended paces

Extended walk

The trot

Working trot

Collected trot

Medium trot

Extended trot

The canter

Working canter

Collected canter

Medium canter

Extended canter

Dressage: lateral work

Most ponies have a 'stiff' side, on which they find certain work more difficult, so they tend to favour their good side as often as they can. You have probably already noticed this in your pony, and certainly will when practising lateral work.

Although it is best to start a new exercise on the rein your pony finds easier, it is important to do every exercise on *both* reins – whether schooling, lungeing or lateral work – to develop suppleness.

As dressage tests become more advanced, the horse is asked to do 'lateral work', or 'work on two tracks' – the hindfeet follow a different track from the forefeet. This happens when he moves sideways, or forward and sideways at the same time, and demonstrates his suppleness, balance and agility.

Turn on the forehand

You have probably asked your horse to go sideways already without noticing it. Think when someone is mucking out a stable with the horse tied up in it. Once they have done one half, they say 'over', and he moves across the stable, making it easier to muck out the other half.

The movement that the horse makes is a sort of 'turn on the forehand', which is one of the first mounted exercises you do when starting lateral work. The turn on the forehand is a useful exercise for three main reasons:

● It teaches your pony to move away from your leg.
● It teaches you to 'blend' the aids given with your legs and your hands.
● It has many everyday uses, such as when opening gates or turning in confined spaces.

In this exercise the pony turns in a half-circle through 180°, so that he changes the direction in which he is facing. It starts from a good, square halt. The outside forefoot marks time (stepping up and down in the same place) and he pivots around it.

The inside forefoot makes a small half-circle around the pivoting outside forefoot, and the hindfeet make a large half-circle to complete the turn.

Giving the aids

The turn on the forehand is made almost entirely with leg aids. The hands do very little. To make a turn to the right (in which you start on the right rein and

Aids for turn on the forehand

1 The start of a turn on the forehand to the left. Make sure the horse is on the bit and listening to you. With your left hand, ask him to look slightly to the left – gently, not pulling, or he may think you want him to step backward.

2 Keep a constant contact on the right rein to prevent the horse stepping forward. Keep your right leg in contact with his side so he doesn't step backward.

end up on the left rein), your pony should first be standing square and on the bit.

Ask him to look slightly to the left by giving little squeezes with the fingers of your left hand, until you can just see his left eye. *Don't pull back* with this hand, or your pony may step backward, which is a serious fault.

Your right hand keeps a steady contact, ready to tell the pony that he is not to step forward. Keep your left leg just at the girth, in contact with his side to keep him up into your hands, and to discourage him from stepping backward.

Your right leg, drawn back a little behind the girth, asks him to turn his hindquarters through the half-circle. Once the turn is complete, ride the pony energetically forward without hesitation. You must ride forward immediate-

Turn on the forehand

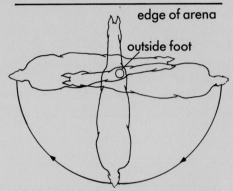

edge of arena

outside foot

In this exercise the pony turns through 180°. Apart from a slight bending of his head (away from the direction in which he is turning, his body remains straight. He pivots around his outside forefoot (shown), the inside forefoot describing a small half-circle and the hindfeet describing a large half-circle.

3 Apply your left leg a little behind the girth, to ask him to turn his hindquarters through the half-circle. Keep your leg on throughout the turn — it should be as fluid as possible, not stopping-and-starting. As soon as you have finished the turn, ride forward straight away. The turn on the forehand is still a *forward* movement, so you don't want him to get the idea that he is going to have a rest when he's finished!

ly so that the pony maintains his forward impulsion, with his hind legs underneath him.

Yielding to the leg

The next exercise that is usually taught in lateral work is 'leg-yielding'. Here the pony is asked to walk or trot forward and sideways at the same time, while remaining parallel to the side of the arena.

An easy way to start this work is to use an exercise that is known as 'yielding to the leg'. It sounds the same as leg-yielding but is not.

Starting on a 20m (66ft) circle (in walk to begin with, and later in trot), ask your pony to make the circle gradually smaller. You could make it a metre (3ft 3in) smaller on each circuit, down to about 12m (39ft).

Keeping the pony bent on the track of the circle – but not with too much bend

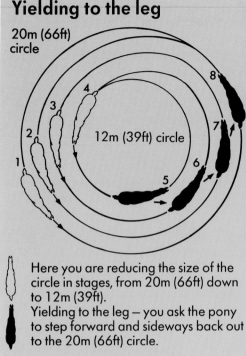

Yielding to the leg

20m (66ft) circle

12m (39ft) circle

Here you are reducing the size of the circle in stages, from 20m (66ft) down to 12m (39ft).
Yielding to the leg – you ask the pony to step forward and sideways back out to the 20m (66ft) circle.

▼ **Yielding to the leg** on a circle. This is a useful exercise for getting the feel of leg-yielding – where your pony moves forward and sideways at the same time.

in his neck – use your inside leg just at the girth to ask him to step forward and sideways back out to the 20m (66ft) circle.

When doing this in trot, it is best to make sitting trot from about the 16m (52ft) circle downward, and when 'yielding to the leg'. This is because it is difficult to rise to the trot on very small circles and still maintain a rhythmical, balanced trot.

When you reach the 20m (66ft) circle start rising again. The work should be done as evenly as possible on both reins. Your pony will almost certainly find it easier one way than the other.

Leg-yielding

When you can do 'yielding to the leg' fairly easily on both reins, try 'leg-yielding' on a straight line, first in walk and then in trot.

It is best if you can start this work in a 20 × 40m (66 × 132ft) arena, so that you can measure exactly what you are doing. On the left rein, start the exercise by making a half 10-metre (33-foot) circle from M or K to bring you on to the centre line (C to A).

Once your pony is moving straight on the centre line, ask him with your inside leg (the left leg on the left rein) to move sideways as well as forward toward the opposite quarter marker K or M. Try to keep the pony parallel to the side of the arena by keeping your outside leg against him to encourage him forward.

Be content with just two or three steps in 'leg-yielding' to start with, then ride the pony straight forward with both legs. As with any new exercise, praise your pony when he achieves what you are asking him to do.

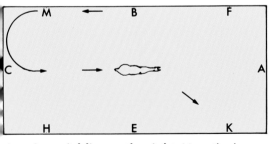

▲ ► **Leg-yielding to the right:** Here the horse is stepping forward and sideways with his off-fore/near-hind diagonal pair at trot. The near-hind is in fact following the track made by the off-fore, which does not happen when trotting in a straight line. The pony's body should remain parallel to the side of the arena throughout the exercise.

Coping with problems: 1

If you watch an unmounted pony in a paddock, you'll notice he moves freely and willingly. His body is relaxed, and he holds his head comfortably and naturally. He shows none of the stiffness or lack of balance that may appear when he's badly ridden.

Tackling the problem

All this should tell you something – most riding problems are caused by riders, past or present! Occasionally, you'll find an unco-operative pony who is simply lazy and anti-social but usually people are to blame.

It is always simpler to *prevent* problems. Many are caused by badly fitting tack that irritates or hurts the pony and makes him play up. Others are caused by weak, ineffectual riding: the pony loses respect for his rider and takes over.

Problems should be stopped as soon as they start or they can quickly get worse. Once they become habits they are very difficult to cure even for an expert. So ask the advice of your instructor when troubles begin – don't wait until they've taken hold.

No pony has all the bad habits which are described here. But problems are common enough for you to gain from learning how to cope – there are few perfect ponies.

Napping

Sometimes called 'jibbing', the pony refuses point-blank to go forward. He 'roots' himself to the spot, maybe braces his forelegs against the ground and may even run backward, kick out or buck. Worst and most dangerous of all, he might rear.

Some ponies nap to test you, others do it with anyone. The pony may be tired, unwell, or confused by your riding. He may be frightened of an obstacle ahead or have something such as his saddle hurting him.

Ask someone knowledgeable to help you check the cause. If fear or confusion are the reason, get another pony to go in front or have someone lead your pony on. Use your legs and seat strongly, speak reassuringly and keep a light contact on the bit.

Thrashing the pony makes him worse although, with a stubborn pony, one good crack behind your leg often works. Try circling the pony, then riding strongly

◄ **Napping:** After stopping dead, the horse may run back, kick, buck or, as here, threaten to rear. The cause may be fear, pain, or weak riding so take expert advice.

❗ PROBLEM ● CHECKLIST

Riding problems stem from a variety of causes that may be nothing to do with the horse, so run through this list of possible reasons before blaming your pony. Ask your vet for advice if you think your stable or pasture management may be at fault.
☐ Is the pony well shod with his hooves properly trimmed?
☐ Does he have any foot disorders that are causing discomfort?
☐ Is he tired? Have you been working him for too long when he's unfit?
☐ Is he well schooled? Is your riding competent or does he need re-training by an instructor?
☐ Are you feeding him enough or, alternatively, giving him too many concentrates?
☐ Does the tack fit properly? Could the pony have a sore mouth?
☐ Does the saddle need re-stuffing? Are you cleaning it regularly so it is supple?

on, or turn round and back him the way you want to go for a short distance.

If the problem continues, the pony should be re-schooled by a competent, sympathetic rider.

Refusing to pass an object

This is usually caused by fear but could develop into stubbornness. If a pony learns that you give up when he comes to a halt, he'll soon stop at everything and go nowhere.

When possible, ask another horse and rider to go first for reassurance. Make your pony follow past the object several times. Ride strongly but not roughly and speak soothingly. Praise him when he goes. If you are in traffic, pass once and continue as if nothing had happened.

If you are alone in traffic, it may be safer to go another way but get a friend to accompany you past the trouble-spot another time. Otherwise, unless you can persuade a passer-by to lead you past, be prepared to sit it out until the pony goes. Keep using your legs strongly and say 'walk on' firmly, but be careful about using your whip – it doesn't usually work.

If you are away from traffic, try turning him round and backing him past or walking in small circles gradu-

ally past it. Praise him when he obeys.

Head shaking

The pony tosses and shakes his head frequently in irritation, not just from feeling good. First check the fit of the bridle as rubbing causes this. The bit too must fit and be comfortable. If the habit is caused by freshness and high spirits, give the pony more exercise and less concentrates (energy foods).

In persistent cases, a standing martingale can help avoid facial injuries to the rider and aid control. Get a vet to check the pony as there are several medical reasons for head shaking. Ride sympathetically and keep your hands steady and light.

Jogging

The pony refuses to walk, going just short of a trot. It's caused by excitement, strange company or being asked to walk too fast. Over-feeding and lack of exercise also start the problem.

You must be patient. *Every* time the pony jogs, gently bring him back to walk at once, otherwise he'll think some jogging is allowed. Use the command 'walk', praising him when he does. Turning him in a small circle can also help. Let him walk slowly on a light

▲ **When confronted** by an unfamiliar object, the pony pricks his ears toward it and stops in his tracks. Be firm and coax him past, even if it takes some time.

Conformation or character?

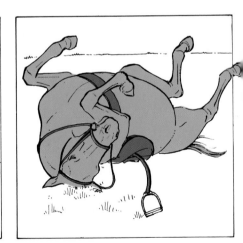

Stargazing
The pony goes with his head and nose high and often with a downward curve to the top of his neck. It may be the way the pony is made, but is also caused by fear of pain in the mouth through heavy hands or an unsuitable bit. Sore backs are another reason so check the tack.

Try a very light bit or a bitless bridle. Use your legs to bring the pony's legs underneath him and encourage him to lower his head.

Stumbling
Horses often trip and stumble if allowed to go sloppily and not ridden up to the bit. Work over trotting poles teaches the pony to look where he's going and to pick up his feet. Stumbling is also caused by faulty hoof-trimming and shoeing, tiredness and foot disorders. Another cause is daisy-cutting, where the pony hardly bends his knees when he moves, and flicks his hooves along close to the ground.

Rolling
Soft ground and water tempt ponies to roll. They may paw first or start buckling at the knees, and some do not hesitate to roll with their rider and saddle on! Keep the pony's head up, sit up and kick on. If his shoulder has gone down, quickly kick off your stirrups and jump off or you could be crushed.

contact so he gets the idea he can take his time. When you trot, make it a proper trot, and he'll gradually improve.

Moving off

Some ponies move off just when you're mounting. Make sure you aren't pulling at the mouth, poking the pony in the ribs or pulling the saddle round.

The instant the pony moves when you're mounting, stop and say 'stand' and put him back in position. Try again and, if he moves, keep trying until you win!

If he moves forward, stand him with his head to the wall. If he moves backward, place his tail to the wall. And if he keeps moving away from you, place his off side to the wall and don't let him go till you're ready.

Kicking

Ponies kick in defence and it's a very difficult vice to cure. The safest remedy is to avoid the hindquarters! Never go behind a known kicker and ask an instructor for advice.

Warn everyone that the pony kicks and keep his quarters turned away from others when riding. Put a red ribbon at the top of his tail. A pony who kicks is quite unsuitable for a child or a novice.

◄ ▲ **The pony** should stay still when you mount and dismount. Moving off is usually because of bad manners, unless *you* are being clumsy or the tack is badly fitted. Don't let him get away with mischief: blocking his path with a wall is a good remedy.

Coping with problems: 2

Some riding problems can be nipped in the bud before they cause real trouble or become bad habits. Other problems are more serious.

What to do

Any pony can be goaded or frightened into misbehaving occasionally. In a problem time, keep your head and your temper. Only tell your pony off *during* the wrong-doing. If you do it afterwards the pony may not connect the harsh words with what he's done wrong, and you'll make him confused.

Shying

Ponies shy (jump suddenly to one side) from playfulness or fear. Too many concentrates (energy foods) and too little work can cause shying, as can poor eyesight. Some ponies shy to play up a weak rider.

In traffic, shying is extremely dangerous. An insecure rider can be thrown and, if the ground is slippery, the pony can fall. If your pony shies, say, to the right, immediately use your right leg strongly with your left rein.

Try to get him to go and inspect whatever he shied at, speaking soothingly at the same time. Carry your whip on the side he shies at – in this case the right.

If you are *certain* that he is not frightened but messing about, give him one smack down the shoulder as you straighten him up, and tell him off.

Ride in a controlled way, and be alert for trouble. But try not to tense up as this could put the pony on edge and actually cause him to shy again.

Bolting/running away

This is extremely frightening and dangerous! It is caused by fear or excitement. However afraid you may feel, don't scream, as this alarms your pony even more. The secret is to keep calm and react quickly, as the longer he keeps running the more difficult it is to stop him.

If you are in an open area, give hard tugs on one rein and turn him in smaller and smaller circles till he has to stop. If you haven't space, bring one hand hard down over the withers and bear down on it to steady yourself, then keep jerking hard upward on the other rein. Repeat on the other side if necessary. Sit up and deep, not forward which encourages even greater speed.

Once you've managed to bring your pony to a halt, do not hit him as he will then associate his punishment with *stopping*. Whatever the reason for bolting – whether it was being fresh, naughty or just frightened – he needs calming down.

You will be more in control if you stay mounted: if you are with a riding group, your instructor may want to ride your ➤

◄ **A pony** may sidestep, shy or rear if frightened by something he sees. As a rider, you can often anticipate an object he may 'spook' at.

➤ **Bolting** is when a pony gets out of control and runs away with his rider.

➤ **Rearing** is a very dangerous vice: the pony could fall over backward and crush the rider.

Do not pull back. Bring your weight forward by leaning up the pony's neck and let the reins go slack.

Ponies who make a habit of rearing cannot be cured.

 GETTING ADVICE
If your pony has reared, don't try any remedies and don't ride him again until you've discussed the vice with your instructor or an expert who knows your pony.

pony back. Heading home might be safest if you've been badly frightened or if your pony is still being difficult. Ride back at a walk – any pace faster just excites your pony. Reassure him by stroking and talking to him as you ride.

If you feel this was an isolated incident, and you can cope, it's better to carry on with your ride. Otherwise your pony might start to think that all he needs to do to get out of a day's work is to play up and he will always get taken home.

Horses have good memories: they are likely to remember the spot where they began to bolt, so next time you are on the same route take another rider with you. Try not to anticipate a problem, relax and ride on as if nothing had happened.

Rearing

Along with true bolting this is the most dangerous vice a horse can have. It is generally caused by pain in the mouth, or fear of it, but sometimes through stubbornness or laziness. Rearers some-

times come over backward, seriously injuring their riders.

If your pony rears, *don't* pull on the reins or he might come over. Get well forward and put your arms round his neck or hold his mane to keep yourself on. *Keep still* and, when he lands, ride strongly forward to prevent him doing it again – ponies have to stop still to rear. Alternatively, dismount.

Bucking

Ponies buck by getting their heads down, arching their backs and jumping up and down. Apart from high spirits, ponies buck to rid themselves of pain or discomfort from tack or rider. So check to see that the saddle and bridle fit well and that you're not doing something that upsets the horse.

If you're on a pony that starts to buck, kick on hard and get his head up with hard jerks on the reins. Don't hit him, it just makes things worse. While he's bucking, tell him off; but as soon as he stops, keep him moving, keep his head up and ignore what happened.

What to do if your pony bucks

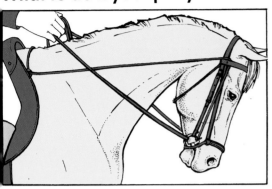

▲ **You can prevent** the first stage of bucking, where the pony gets his head down, by fitting 'grass reins'. Tie a length of binder twine to each bit ring. Pass the twine up through the browband loops, then to the D-rings on each side of the saddle. Make sure the twine is short enough to stop the pony's head from going below the level of his withers. Some experts feel grass reins make ponies bolt as they're unused to them, so have a supervisor there when you fit the reins.

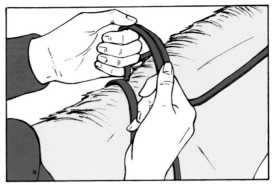

▲ **When riding a pony that bucks,** start your ride by making a bridge with your reins. It braces your fall forward against the pony's neck and because the reins are shorter, it stops the pony's head from going down. Hold the reins as normal, then double the spare rein above the withers: take the rein above your left thumb and hold it under the fourth finger of your right hand. Now take the spare rein above your right thumb and hold it under the fourth finger of your left hand.

▼ **Some ponies play up** to rid themselves of their rider: but there can be a practical reason too — such as a badly fitting saddle that pinches.

Your first hack

▼ **Going on a hack** is one of riding's great treats.

Hacking is one of the most delightful aspects of riding. It makes a refreshing change from lessons in the school and is a reward for all the previous hard work. A hack builds up your confidence in the saddle and allows you to explore the countryside. Also, going out and about gives you a chance to get to know more thoroughly the pony you ride.

Preparation

For your first hack the riding school will assess your ability and match you to a reliable horse, probably the one you always ride. There will also be experienced riders at the head and tail of the ride.

Dress for safety and comfort and, before setting off, carefully check over the pony's tack. If he is a little fresh (excited), or has not been ridden for a while, it is best to walk him round the school for a few minutes to settle him down.

Setting off

When you set out, begin in walk, until the pony's muscles are warmed up. The walk should be controlled, not sloppy. If you are with a group of riders, keep up with the person in front of you – but don't get too close. Aim to keep at least one horse's length away. If you allow your pony to nip at the quarters of the horse in front, you could be on the receiving end of a rather unpleasant kick! Also, if you ride abreast, leave one pony's width between you and the pony beside you.

Use this opening walk as a chance to practise some of the things learned in the school – leg and hand position, balanced seat, straight back and a gentle contact with the mouth.

A steady walk is a good discipline. You'll find that some ponies may need encouraging, others holding back, particularly on the homeward stretch.

Road work

Most hacks involve some road work before you reach tracks and bridleways so make sure you know the rules of the road. When you are learning to ride, you will almost certainly be given a traffic-proof pony. You should never take this for granted, however. It's a confidence-builder to know you could cope effectively with an animal that is traffic-shy.

If your horse does play up, he may be genuinely afraid. In this case you should be patient but firm. If possible, let him have a good look at what is frightening him, while patting him reassuringly to soothe him.

Stay alert

Make sure you are in control of the pony before venturing into open countryside. After being in a riding school a pony can be excitable. A large ride might be split into groups of two and three riders, to avoid all the ponies charging off. Horses love to race, and can get worked up, but most stop if they are turned in a circle or if they get ahead of the other animals.

A good place for a first canter is up a hill – it's unlikely that the pony can run away with you, and it strengthens his muscles. Go downhill at the walk until you're a very experienced rider. Remember, never canter on hard ground or after heavy rain, as the conditions may be slippery and dangerous.

Also, don't let your pony nibble at grass while you're out. This can become a habit which is difficult to stop.

HACK FACTS
An hour is quite enough for your first hack. Later you can build up to longer outings, perhaps going out for the whole afternoon and taking a picnic with you. Remember that both you and your pony have to be fit enough to manage this sort of ride!

Longer hacks take you deeper into the countryside, off well-established paths. So make sure you know where you can and cannot go.

◄ **Being on horseback** means you see aspects of the countryside that you wouldn't see on foot. You are higher up than normal and so get a better view — and animals aren't as frightened of horses, so you see more of them too.

► **Returning home** at a walk ensures that you and the pony slowly relax. This means you both arrive at the stables calm and cool.

▼ **Out in the open** you have freedom to move. Once you've checked to make sure the ground is suitable, you can begin to canter.

Enjoying yourself

One of the pleasures of hacking is that it gives you a much better view of the countryside than walking does. You can see more because you are higher up than if you were on foot. Also, animals such as deer or badgers, who may be frightened by people on foot, are less likely to be disturbed by horses.

Watch your pony and see how he responds to your instructions out of the school. Note his reactions to the countryside – you'll learn a lot about him!

Another benefit is the opportunity to learn new skills in a natural setting. What was daunting in the school becomes easy when hacking – if the whole ride moves off at a canter, your pony will want to canter too. You'll be caught up in the excitement and go, almost without thinking about it. Paces and movements learnt during lessons happen naturally – and sometimes unpredictably – keeping you and the pony interested and keen.

Back at the stables

☐ **Walk the last half mile,** especially if it has been tiring. This lets your pony cool down and relax. You could even dismount, loosen the girth, run the irons up the leathers and lead him some of the way home. It helps ease *your* stiffness too!

☐ **Once home, thank your pony** and remove his tack. If the weather is warm and the pony is still hot, you can sponge him down with water. On a cool day, rub him down with handfuls of hay. Make sure he is dry, especially his ears, croup and neck.

☐ **Muddy or stony ground** when you're out on a hack means you must pick out the pony's hooves on your return. And if you've walked through thick undergrowth, check him thoroughly for any small scratches.

☐ **Never allow a pony to drink cold water immediately:** this could chill his stomach and cause colic. As he will be thirsty, give him a few mouthfuls of tepid water, and only let him drink his fill when he is dry and cool.

☐ **A feed for your pony** is the final task before you have your own tea!

All of these 'rules' are simply common sense — but they are important. Remembering them contributes to your enjoyment and the pony's well-being.

On the road

Road sense is essential for every rider. Staying safe is a mixture of commonsense, courtesy and alertness. You need to anticipate the movements of motorists and to show clearly where you intend to go.

Safety on the road

Before setting out, check that your horse's tack is safe. Make sure that his shoes are in good condition because badly worn shoes provide little or no grip. Never ride on the road without a saddle and bridle.

If you do a lot of roadwork, you may want to invest in knee boots for your pony. They protect the horse's legs if he falls on a hard surface. You could also ask your farrier to put some small road studs on the shoes to improve his grip.

You should wear sensible clothes and take your riding whip with you if you have one. Always carry your whip in your right hand because this will be on the outside close to the traffic. You can then encourage your horse to move toward the edge of the road away from the traffic when necessary.

Road awareness

Be aware of other road-users and take extra care to control your horse. Even well-behaved horses are unpredictable in traffic.

Always ride along the side of the road, as close to the kerb as possible. If you can, ride on grass verges, but keep a sharp lookout for dangerous hidden hazards such as drainage ditches and broken glass.

Never ride on pavements or footways. They're intended for pedestrians and the sight of a horse blocking the route can be frightening and dangerous to small children and adults alike.

No matter how tempting an open road or a verge may look, keep to a steady walk or trot. If you canter and your horse suddenly shies you may lose control. Fast paces are also more damaging to the horse's legs and feet on hard surfaces. In any case, you should never gallop on a horse wearing knee boots because it can hurt him.

Whenever possible, avoid riding in the dark. Never ride in fog or mist because you can't see – or be seen easily.

◄ **Riding in single file** is safest, even on quiet country roads. But if you do want to ride two abreast, always be ready to go back into single file if the road narrows or traffic approaches.

▼ **Wear bright clothing** when riding on roads, to make it easy for drivers to spot you as they approach.

Obey the rules regarding crossings, traffic lights, one-way streets and road signs. They apply to you just as much as to motorized traffic, whether you are riding or leading a horse.

Always wear a hard hat. After sunset, wear light or reflective clothing. Take special care at railway crossings.

Because the road rules vary so greatly in the United States, it is best to check with some local authority before riding or leading a horse on a highway. Hand signals may not always have the same meaning from one area to another.

Improving your roadcraft

▲ **Riding and road safety tests** are run by most local authorities. If you ride regularly in built-up areas it's a good idea to take tests to improve your roadcraft. You can get further details from your local police station, riding school or riding club.

The tests involve all aspects of road safety including turning, stopping and coping with disturbances. Obstacles will be put in your way to test both you and your pony's steadiness (as above). The most important thing is to carry on calmly.

ROAD SAFETY

When riding on roads, bear in mind these golden rules for everyone's safety and enjoyment.

☐ Wear a hard hat, correct and safe clothing and use well-fitting tack.

☐ Never ride on the road without a saddle and bridle.

☐ Know and obey the rules of the road.

☐ Always ride as close to the kerb (curb) as possible.

☐ Never ride along footways and pavements, or sidewalks.

☐ Be considerate to other road-users.

☐ Stay alert – keep your attention on the road at all times.

☐ Give correct and clear signals.

☐ Avoid very busy roads.

☐ Thank drivers who slow down for you.

☐ Avoid riding in the dark. Never ride in fog or mist.

☐ Ask permission to pass other riders in front of you before overtaking them.

Signalling

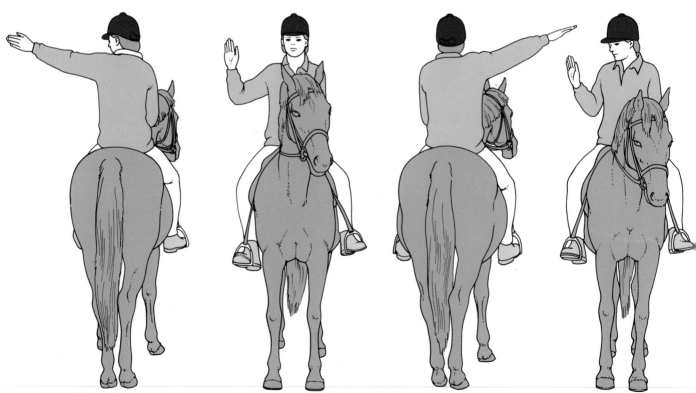

▲ **To turn left,** extend your left arm. To turn right, extend your right arm in the same way.

▲ **To stop oncoming traffic,** hold up your right hand with your palm toward the traffic.

▲ **To slow traffic down,** hold out your arm closest to the traffic and slowly wave it up and down.

▲ **To thank a driver,** hold up your right hand with your arm slightly bent and smile politely.

Riding in a group

When you go out riding with a group of friends, the riders at each end are responsible for giving all the hand signals. Position the most reliable horses at the front and back. Divide groups of more than six into two rides so that you don't hold up the traffic.

If the road is wide enough, riding two abreast encourages passing vehicles to move slowly and give you more room. If it narrows ahead, be prepared to move back into single file. Don't become so absorbed in your conversation that you take no notice of your surroundings.

If you want to overtake riders in front of you, always check with them first so that you don't startle their ponies.

Turning

To turn left, place the reins and whip in your right hand and hold your left arm out to your side at shoulder height.

When turning right or passing a stationary vehicle, place the reins and whip in your left hand and hold your right arm out at shoulder height. Remember that when passing a vehicle on your side of the road you should give right of way to oncoming traffic.

Giving signals

Before altering your course indicate clearly to other road-users. Check in front and behind first, signal clearly and allow drivers time to react before you move. Always thank those who slow down – this will encourage them to be more considerate to other riders.

Don't signal with a whip in your hand. It can frighten the horse and confuse other road-users.

When a car is uncertain whether to overtake you or not, beckon it on with your right hand *provided that the road ahead is clear.*

To ask a driver to stop, hold your right hand up, palm facing toward him. Before doing this make sure that the road is clear. If you need to slow traffic down, hold out your arm nearest the traffic and wave it up and down.

◄ **At a road junction,** look both left and right, wait until all's clear and then proceed.

▲ **Signal in plenty of time** to warn approaching drivers of your exact movements.

Night riding 1: the horse

If you are at work or at school, early morning or evening are the only times you can ride a pony. When you are away all day, your pony should ideally be turned out during the daylight hours and night riding confined to an indoor school or floodlit arena. But if this is impossible, choose quiet, well-lit roads to ride on, and make sure you and your pony are visible to other road users.

Show up in the dark

Light-coloured clothing, reflective accessories and lights are the key to being seen at night.

For the horse, the most essential item is a sturdy stirrup light clipped to the right stirrup, showing a clear white light to the front and a strong red light to the back. The types which strap to your boot are quite good but can sometimes swivel out of position.

Most saddlers sell stirrup lights, either in their shops or by mail order, so you should have no difficulty in getting them. Always keep spare batteries to hand and check the strength of the light before you use it.

Reflecting the light

Other items consist of clothing (exercise sheets), bandages and stick-on strips for the bridle. These are made of material which reflects the light from motorists' headlights or from any street lighting.

Reflective white is the most easily seen colour at night, but reflective yellow, pink or orange are all good.

Exercise sheets made of lightweight mesh cover the quarters and back, like an ordinary rug, but go on under the saddle. By wearing a light-coloured one your pony will be warm and visible.

Reflective bandages should go on the pony's two right legs – closest to the middle of the road – or on all four. Some firms even sell reflective boots.

Stick-on strips are also available for parts of the bridle – cheekpieces, browband and noseband. The adhesive does not damage the leather and the strips are easy to put on and take off again.

GROUP SAFETY
If a group of you exercise together, try to put the palest pony at the back of the line and the next palest at the front. They are the easiest to see.

► **Make your horse clearly visible** with a brightly coloured exercise sheet, reflective strips and stirrup lights.

WHERE TO RIDE
Always ride on quiet, well-lit roads at night.

Bridleways are inadvisable because neither you nor the pony can see well enough. Unlit lanes, particularly winding ones with high hedges, are extremely dangerous. Apart from being unable to see your way, motorized traffic cannot see you around the corners.

Busy main roads are also dangerous (day or night) unless they have a proper riding track.

Night riding 2: the rider

Once you have kitted out the horse for night riding, you need to equip yourself. Your clothing, whether riding or leading a pony in the dark, should be as pale as possible. Some items should also be reflective.

Clothing and lights

Reflective clothing for riders includes hat covers and bands, tabards, and arm and leg bands. These are all available from good riding equipment shops, saddlers or cycling shops. The more reflective items you wear the better.

When leading a pony, it's a good idea to carry a lantern-type light. The type available from motoring or camping shops showing a red light to the back and a white one to the front is suitable.

If you want to keep a hand free, you can get a light that straps on to your arm. Alternatively, get two lanterns and rig up a harness from binder twine to hold one light on your chest and one on your back.

Remember to lead the pony in his bridle. This gives you greater control over the pony than a headcollar does. Stick reflective strips on the bridle.

Ideally, get someone to accompany you and carry the lantern, so you have both hands free to control the pony.

★ **LIGHTS ON**

One source of safety equipment often overlooked by riders is cycling shops. These sell a good range of equipment which is reflective as well as illuminated.

You can buy belts and cross-sashes with little lights fitted along every few centimetres and operated from a neat, waterproof battery unit. You can also buy wrist lights to make sure your signals are clearly seen.

★ **LIGHT FANTASTIC**

The advantage of lights as opposed to reflectors or reflective clothing is that they are visible many metres or yards ahead. Reflective items are only picked up in car headlights when the vehicle is comparatively near. Wear lights *and* reflectors to be on the safe side.

► **Being seen** is essential when you ride in the dark. Wearing reflectors and lights makes you clearly visible to other road users.

In the country

One of the best ways to see the countryside is on horseback. By following the country code of courtesy and commonsense, you'll fully enjoy riding through open fields and along bridleways.

Choosing your route

If you're new to an area, find out exactly where you are allowed to ride before setting off.

Ask your local riding school or club for information about good hacking country in your district. Also, look at some local maps to find out exactly where the bridleways are.

If there are only a few bridleways near you, ask local farmers if you can ride across their land. Provided that you're a responsible rider, they may well agree, particularly at slack times of the year – just after crops have been harvested for example. Whatever you do, never risk damaging farmland or trespassing over other people's property.

Taking care

Courteous riding in the countryside is just as important as it is on the road. Other people enjoying the countryside deserve consideration, too. When riding on farmland, there are several things to remember.

● Although you should keep to bridleways, try not to ride straight through herds of grazing animals – skirt around them, breaking away from the path, if necessary.

● If the bridleway passes through a field of crops but the track is not well defined, ride carefully around the edge of the field.

● Always leave gates as you found them. There's nothing more annoying for a farmer than his herd escaping through a gate left open. And he'll never want riders on his land again!

● People out walking may be frightened of horses, so slow down when passing them. Always greet people cheerfully.

● If the ground is wet, try to avoid

◄ **The joy of riding** through the countryside far from the bustle of busy roads can be enormous. You can canter across fields or take your time to enjoy the beautiful scenery.

◄ **Always take great care** and pay attention to your surroundings when riding in the country. You may come across hazards like a low branch of a tree. Be sure to duck in plenty of time!

❗ ALTERNATIVE PATHS
If lots of horses use a bridleway, the track can get damaged. You may see a sign asking riders not to use the path until it recovers. Although it's annoying to change your course, remember that it's for your benefit in the long run – take an alternative path.

Country hazards

☐ Make sure you are aware of the hazards on unknown ground. You may come across rabbit holes, uneven and rutted land, overhanging branches or ditches. If the ground looks really bad, check the land ahead for safety and retrace your footsteps, before starting to canter.

☐ Whatever you do, don't jump fences or hedges as they may conceal strands of barbed wire. In any case, you might damage the boundary and fences and the farmer could prosecute you.

☐ If a bridleway is blocked by, say, a fallen tree, always ask the owner for permission before attempting to clear it. Otherwise, a fallen tree trunk does provide a wonderful natural obstacle to practise your jumping skills!

☐ If you have to ride along or cross any rural roads, be careful. Although they are often narrow and twisty, there's usually little traffic, so passing motorists may be going faster than usual. They will probably not expect a horse ahead!

☐ Listen out for the sound of an approaching car and be ready to move across to the edge of the road and, if there is one, on to the verge. Before crossing a road look right, left and right again to make sure that it is clear before moving briskly.

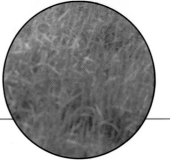

cantering. Although it's fun, it churns up the ground and makes the way difficult for other riders to pass.

Riding in comfort

As with all other aspects of riding, pay attention to both safety and comfort. Wear a hard hat and sensible footwear and check that all your horse's tack is securely fastened and in good condition.

Since weather can be changeable, even in the middle of the summer, take a lightweight waterproof mac – tie it to the D-rings across the front or back of the saddle.

Put a headcollar and lead-rope beneath the bridle so you can tie the horse up safely if you stop on the way.

On longer rides take a saddle-bag or a numnah with pockets for carrying things. A map, a hoof pick to take stones out of your horse's hooves and a pocket first-aid kit, containing a bandage and plasters, are all useful. A piece of string also helps for emergency tack repairs. And why not take some sandwiches for a picnic – but make sure you bring your litter home with you!

Courtesy code

▼ Follow these simple do's and don'ts every time you ride in the country.

DO'S	DON'TS
* Keep to marked bridleways	* Don't trespass – ask farmers before riding across their land
* Close gates after riding through them	
* Ride at a steady walk or trot in wet weather	* Don't break down hedges or damage fences by jumping them
* Be polite and considerate to walkers and other riders	* Avoid riding through groups of grazing animals
* Look out for natural hazards such as rabbit holes and ditches	* Don't drop your litter – take it home with you

▲ **Natural obstacles** such as fallen tree trunks can be fun to jump and are excellent for basic jumping practice.

◄ **When riding through fields,** move quietly – and slowly – around and past livestock. You may alarm the animals and, if they become panicky, your horse may get frightened as well.

Going through a gate

◄ **Always approach** a gate at a walk and position your horse sideways on. Undo the latch with the hand that's closest to the gate while holding the reins in your other hand.

► **Pull the gate** slowly toward you. Ask the horse to move backward and push his hindquarters around with your legs so that the gate doesn't hit him.

◄ **Hold on to the gate** as you ride through. Then turn the horse round so that he is parallel with the gate and fasten the latch securely.

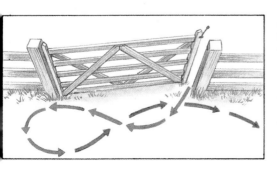

At first you will need to make a complete turn after you have ridden through a gate (left). But, when you and your pony are more experienced, you will find that you can turn on the forehand (right).

Tackling different terrains

In the wild, a horse has to travel across all sorts of terrain – steep hills, running water, stony tracks or boggy pastures. But not all domesticated horses are familiar with such changing landscapes and a good rider knows how to help.

Up and down hills

Hillwork can be demanding – even for a fairly fit pony – and, as a rider, you must use your commonsense about the kind of climbs you ask your pony to attempt. On any ascent, you should lean forward in the saddle and keep no more than a light contact with the pony's mouth.

Similarly, for a gentle downward incline, just lean back slightly. On a steeper slope, position your weight further back and try to help the pony keep his footing. If you feel your balance going, don't hang on to the reins: use the front of the saddle to steady yourself.

Many ponies are quite happy when going uphill but are very wary of coming back down again. Watch what is happening – especially if you are approaching the top of a short, steep bank. A pony may decide that, rather than risk slipping, the best answer is to jump straight off – and an inattentive rider can easily get left behind!

Downhill on roads

Riding downhill on roads is a different matter. Think about the steepness of the hill and the condition of the road surface. Worn roads tend to become slippery and it is unsafe to go any faster than a walk.

Worn shoes on slippery roads double the danger so make sure that there is plenty of 'tread' on your pony's shoes. If you have to do a lot of roadwork, you may want to have road studs fitted to them. Ask for expert advice first: studs can unbalance a horse and so lead to leg problems later on.

Stony ground

Hill tracks are often stony so, although ponies are usually very sure-footed, keep to a walk to avoid the risk of unnecessary injury.

Once you've ridden along such a path, stop your pony, dismount and check his feet to see no stones have lodged in his hooves. You may find you need a hoof pick – so always carry one just in case! When you get home, check your pony's hooves again and make sure he has not injured his legs.

Streams, rivers and lakes

Before you ride alongside – or across – a stream or river, find out whether it is safe to do so. Shallow waters can suddenly flow into deep pools and broad, flat river beds may be covered with slippery pebbles.

The approach is also important. Do

▼ **Bridleways** through grassland are ideal riding country. Look out for slippery mud and puddles concealing ruts and potholes if it has recently rained.

you have to go down a slippery, stony bank or through a shady stretch of woodland? Ponies dislike going from light into shade. If there are trees along the bank, there may be shafts of sunlight filtering through, making patches of light and dark on the water.

Such a scene may be appealing to the rider but very frightening to the pony. If you have a nervous pony – especially one who is naturally suspicious of water – the best way to overcome his fear is to take a companion who can ride with you and lead the way.

You should also watch out for warning signs from a pony who *enjoys* being in water and may be tempted to roll in it. If he starts to splash or paw at the water surface, get his head up with quick, firm jerks on the reins then sit up and kick on – otherwise he will probably take an untimely dip!

▼ **Cantering** through shallow water on a gently shelving sandy beach is exhilarating and good fitness training. But don't push your pony through soft sand.

◄ **Approach lakes and ponds** with care so you can check how deep the water is and what the bottom is like. Make sure you are in control of the pony – even if, as here, he has just had a drink.

► **Flooded fields** should be taken at a cautious pace as boggy ground is stressful for the horse's legs. Check your pony's shoes afterwards.

Puddles and mud

Puddles on tracks or roads are not usually a problem, but try to keep to the dry parts of the road as the water may conceal a pothole or broken paving stones – both of which could seriously hurt your pony.

After heavy rain, the countryside can become very boggy. Badly poached or muddy tracks are generally closed by landowners. Even if you have permission to ride on grassland or around the borders of crop fields, you should respect the land and avoid churning it up for no good reason.

From your pony's point of view, heavy ground places extra strain on his muscles, tendons and joints. Before you go over a boggy field, ask yourself if you are being unfair to your pony. The fitter he is, the better he is able to cope, but you must be aware that problems could crop up.

Boggy ground is also the chief culprit for pulling off shoes, even newly fitted ones, and a loose shoe can easily cause injury to the foot or opposite leg.

Fun by the seaside

If you are lucky enough to live near the sea, you have a wonderful 'all-weather' area, excellent for training or schooling. Racehorse trainers use miles of sandy beach as gallops, and the sand close beside the water's edge, where the water

◄ **Steep, stony uphills** make going tough for the pony. Watch out for stones lodging in your pony's hooves. Keep to a walk and lean forward to take the weight off his back. The lead rider here should have more rein contact.

Your position for hillwork

When you go downhill, sit upright and even lean back a little. Keep a positive contact with the pony's mouth to help him balance. If he loses his balance he could stumble and fall, particularly if you are on slippery grass or muddy ground.

If the descent is steep, give the pony more rein but be ready to tighten the contact again as soon as you reach the bottom so that you stay in control. On a difficult slippery bank, the pony may tuck his hocks right underneath him and more or less slide down.

To climb hills, a pony needs to use his back and quarter muscles and to breathe faster. You can help him by leaning forward in the saddle, keeping a light, even contact through the reins to your pony's mouth.

Do not use his mouth to balance yourself – take hold of a piece of mane to help you stay in a forward position if necessary.

❗ HOLES AND BURROWS
Be extra careful if you know you are on ground where burrowing animals have been. You could have a nasty fall if your pony's leg goes down a hole, particularly if you are riding downhill or moving at speed.

▼ Sunset dream: What could be more perfect than a holiday evening's ride along a deserted beach?

is shallow, provides just the right kind of going for horses who are used to racing on turf.

As with other terrain, you must know your beach, particularly the height and time of the tides, and whether any part becomes cut off or covered at high tide. Find out how the sand differs over the beach: whether it becomes deep and soft, perhaps at the bottom of sand dunes, or whether there are large flat areas of rock covered by shallow sand.

Consider other beach users, and ride there only when you can be sure you are not creating a nuisance. On the other hand, look out for litter that beach users leave behind – broken bottles, can ring-pulls and sharp tin – which could hurt your pony.

On any kind of different going, be considerate – to your pony and to other land users. Before you ask your pony to take you through deep, boggy fields or soft sand, think how *your* legs might feel if you got off and walked. Sometimes, in difficult conditions, or to give your pony a rest, you could do just that and lead your pony beside you.

Riding in all weathers

It would be lovely if every day were perfect riding weather – calm, sunny and with just a cooling breeze. Unfortunately, such days are rare. You often have to ride in adverse conditions, and sometimes the weather changes dramatically while you are out.

Natural reactions

Although horses naturally live out in the open, they are not immune to extreme weather and like to shelter from it. They stand with their tails to the wind and whatever it brings with it – rain, sleet or hail. They detest having their heads to the weather and can become difficult if forced to go into it.

◄ Riding in the rain is best avoided, but when you get caught in a downpour you can shield both yourself and your pony with a long waterproof mac.

Caught in the rain

Do not set out in very heavy rain: your pony will dislike it and might become difficult. If you get caught in a shower, try to find shelter and/or let your pony stand with his tail to the rain – unless it's coming straight down!

When you set off for a long ride in cold weather and there's a chance it might rain or sleet heavily, fit a waterproof exercise sheet to your pony and roll up a waterproof mac for yourself. You could tie it to the D-rings of your saddle, but dismount to put it on and take it off, unless there is someone with you to hold your pony. Or, you could wear a long mac to keep you – and your pony's back – dry.

When you get home, you need to dry the pony off, particularly if it's cold as well as wet. Thatch him (with straw under a rug) and dry his ears, neck and legs before rugging him up as you usually do. Change to dry rugs when his coat is no longer wet.

Lightning storms

Like people, some ponies are frightened of thunder and lightning. Never set out for a ride in a storm. If you are out, and a storm blows up, make sure you get home as quickly as you reasonably can. If you are too far from home, try to seek shelter, perhaps at a farm, or in a half-empty hay barn.

Lightning is attracted to the tallest object in an area, so it's best to find safe shelter near *small* trees, a shrubbery, or an orchard. If you are on a hill, go to the bottom of it.

Keep out of water: water is a good conductor of electricity and the current will go through you too.

If you are in a flat area with no trees, you are the tallest object – and lightning may be attracted to you. It's best to dismount. If lightning and thunder occur at the same moment, it means that the storm is overhead. Crouch down and stay low until the worst of the weather has moved on.

Riding on very hot days can exhaust your pony. If he is listless and sweating a lot, find some shade and water for him to drink. Scoop *warm* (never ice-cold) water between his ears, down his neck and on his shoulders to help cool him: cold water causes muscle cramps. Let him rest, then walk gently home. If he does not improve, call the vet.

► **Hot weather:** Try to avoid midday when the sun is at its hottest. Early morning or late afternoon is cooler, and you can enjoy yourselves without risk of sunstroke.

▼ **At summer shows,** take advantage of available shade in between classes.

Coping with the sun

Just like people, ponies can suffer from sunstroke. If they have had too much sun, they will be weak, start to stagger, and may pant dog-like breaths as they try to cool down.

But provided the work is not long and hard, horses come to no harm. It is when the weather is humid and 'muggy' that trouble begins: a pony cannot evaporate away his excess body heat because the surrounding air is too damp. You can help your pony by putting an absorbent quilted cotton numnah under the saddle to soak up excess sweat. An absorbent girth made from material such as lamp-

wick (thick woven webbing) is also more comfortable. Don't attempt long or fast work in such conditions.

Dehydration

The main problem with riding in hot conditions is dehydration: the pony sweats much more and needs water to replace what he has lost. Plan your route so you can get him to drinking places: make sure the water at these points is good. Let your pony have one short drink each time (about four or five swallows). You can count by watching the underside of his neck.

Stand the pony still for a moment, or

at least go no faster than a walk, for about five minutes afterwards. When you get home, give your pony a similar drink, but do not allow him his fill until he is cool. Offer him short drinks every 15 minutes until he has had enough. Leave him a supply of water.

Battling with the wind

Horses and ponies hate wind. They naturally stand with their backs to it to shield their sensitive heads. If the wind is very strong, it's best not to ride. If the wind doesn't amount to an actual gale, find sheltered routes and don't interfere too much with your pony's head – he'll want to lower it against the wind to protect himself.

If the weather is cold as well as windy, a clipped, finely bred horse needs an exercise sheet, and you should wear a windproof jacket yourself.

Snow and ice

Most ponies enjoy fresh snow. If you are going to ride in it, pack your pony's hooves with grease – old cooking fat, soft soap or melted candle wax – to stop the snow balling up in his feet. Ask your farrier whether he thinks road studs, or frost nails (which give a good grip on ice), would be advisable.

Any snow disguises the ground, so pick an area which you know is even with no sudden pit holes or dips. Avoid deep snow as, like deep water, it unbalances your pony and makes the going strenuous for him. If you suddenly find yourself in deep snow, let him go at his own pace. You should also avoid frozen, crusty snow, which can cut a pony's legs.

In icy conditions, lay down exercise tracks and rings around the stable yard and ride on those. Used bedding, ashes, sand and grit are all suitable and stop the pony falling over and hurting himself – or you!

Do not deliberately set out on roads you know to be icy. If you come upon an unexpected patch, quit (take your feet out of) your stirrups, so you can leap off quickly if the pony slips. Let the pony pick his own way, and stay quite still in the saddle. Give the pony his head so he can balance.

Foggy conditions

Never go out in fog or mist. If it comes down while you are out, turn for home using the best-lit route. In autumn and winter, clip a strong stirrup light to your right iron. If fog does come down, you can switch it on while you are getting home. Wear reflective clothing so motorists can see you better. While a stirrup light helps in an emergency, it's much better to avoid problems and ride at home on an exercise track.

★ RIDING IN HAIL

It can be very painful to get caught in a hailstorm. Allow your pony to shelter if at all possible, rather than pushing on (you'll probably be glad to take cover yourself!).

If there's nowhere to go, let him stand with his tail to the direction of the hail, as he would if left to himself. Where hail builds up on the ground, it can be slippery, so ride as if it were ice.

▼ **Snow and ice:** Frost nails or road studs help your pony keep his feet, but avoid slippery ice patches when you can.

Going for a day ride

One of the greatest pleasures of riding is a day out on horseback with friends. A little planning beforehand means you and the ponies enjoy the long picnic ride in safety.

Forward planning

The first thing you should do when organizing a whole-day ride is plan the route on a map. You should not attempt to do more than 34km (20 miles) – and even this distance assumes your pony is fit for long, steady riding.

A horse or pony on an average hack travels at about 9km (5½ miles) an hour, so 34km (20 miles) would take some four hours. Add on another hour for lunch, and a bit more for rest breaks on the way, and plan to be away for no more than six hours. Aim to ride for two and a half hours before stopping for lunch.

Ask somebody with a car to drive over your planned route with you, so you can check it is suitable. This also gives you an opportunity to choose a good picnic spot – with grazing and water for the ponies.

Discuss with your friends who is goin to join the ride. Don't take total inexperienced riders who won't be ab to cope. All the ponies must be fit, n too fat or too thin, and none should under five years old (the distance wou be too much for them). Try to sele ponies whose paces match. A fligh erratic pony with long strides, for exa ple, only upsets the day.

Now is also the time to choose t group's guide – someone efficient at m reading and able to use a compass.

Preparations

Check your pony's shoes – good sho are vitally important at any time, b you don't want the slightest sign of we if you're planning a long ride.

The evening before the ride, cle your tack and check it thoroughly f any sign of damage. The tack must used – this is not the occasion for tryi out new equipment which may cha Make sure the bridle and saddle correctly and the numnah and girth a clean.

Before you leave, you must, for sa

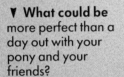

▼ **What could be** more perfect than a day out with your pony and your friends?

Plan well in advance so on the day you can concentrate on having fun.

's sake, tell somebody exactly where you are going, who is with you, and the time you expect to be back.

On the morning of the ride, feed your pony at least two hours before you set off. Your breakfast, too, should be eaten long before you leave, and should not be greasy or fried, which might make you feel queasy.

Front and rear files

Before you set off, appoint a sensible front rider, or 'leading file'. When the ride is proceeding one behind the other, leading file has to keep a wary eye out for broken bottles, rusty cans, rabbit holes or boggy ground.

The leading file should call out the danger, for example 'beware glass' or 'hole on the left', so that everyone can hear. If there are a lot of you and the people at the back can't hear, pass the message on down the line.

The leading file also sets the pace, which should be comfortable for *all* of you so that no-one has to struggle to keep up. At the front of the ride, you always have to think about the others

behind. For example, don't start cantering on open grass as soon as you emerge from a wood – the others may still be ducking low branches!

Tuck the least experienced riders in the middle, and have another responsible rider for 'rear file'. The rear file warns the others of hazards from behind, such as overtaking vehicles on roads, and uses hand signals to drivers.

The rear file is also responsible for keeping the ride together so you don't end up being too spread out. He or she should tell leading file to slow the pace if people are getting left behind.

Although you should keep close together, don't tread on each other's heels – keep your distance from the pony in front. And don't just rely on the lead and rear files to point out any dangerous objects or overtaking traffic: this is a joint responsibility, and part of good riding is to be alert.

Thoughtful riding

A fun day out is no excuse for careless or sloppy riding. In fact, on a day like this it is more important than usual to think

about your hands and seat.

Lolling about in the saddle and being careless with your hands over such a long period of time makes a pony extra tired and sore. Don't continually nag the pony with your legs, or drag on his mouth while you turn round to chat or admire the scenery.

Adopt a light, balanced seat and use your hips, knees and ankles as shock absorbers. Avoid sitting trot, and change the diagonal every so often in rising trot. Take the forward position when you are cantering, and vary the leading leg.

Pacing yourselves

The ride is not a sweaty dash across country, jumping everything in sight. It involves plenty of walking, steady trotting periods, a few short canters and no galloping.

Let the others know if you want to jump an obstacle, so you don't upset the other ponies by suddenly rushing off.

Go down hills slowly – especially if they are long and steep. Lean forward going up the hills, and give the pony enough rein to stretch.

Walk on stony, rough or rutted tracks, and keep to a walk or slow trot on the roads. Only canter on soft ground in safe places, and *never* on verges next to roads.

Homeward bound

Walk at least the last mile of the ride so you arrive home relaxed. Allow for this when planning your timetable for the day – you should never have to rush back to be on time.

When you get home, thank your pony for his hard work by making much of him. Check him over for any little injuries. Wipe off sweat patches, brush him down and pick out his feet. When you have done all this, give him his feed.

► **Allow your pony** to drink a little on the ride. If he has nothing to drink all day, and is then given gallons on arriving home, he may get colic.

**! LOSING
• YOUR WAY**

If you get lost, don't panic. Steer a straight line and you will eventually find someone to tell you where you are. Also, ponies have a good sense of direction – given his head, your pony may well point his nose for home!

▼ **A selection of items** to take with you in your saddle bags.

reflective belt

coin for telephone

saddle bag

picnic lunch

hoof pick

map

first-aid kit

penknife

string

headcollar

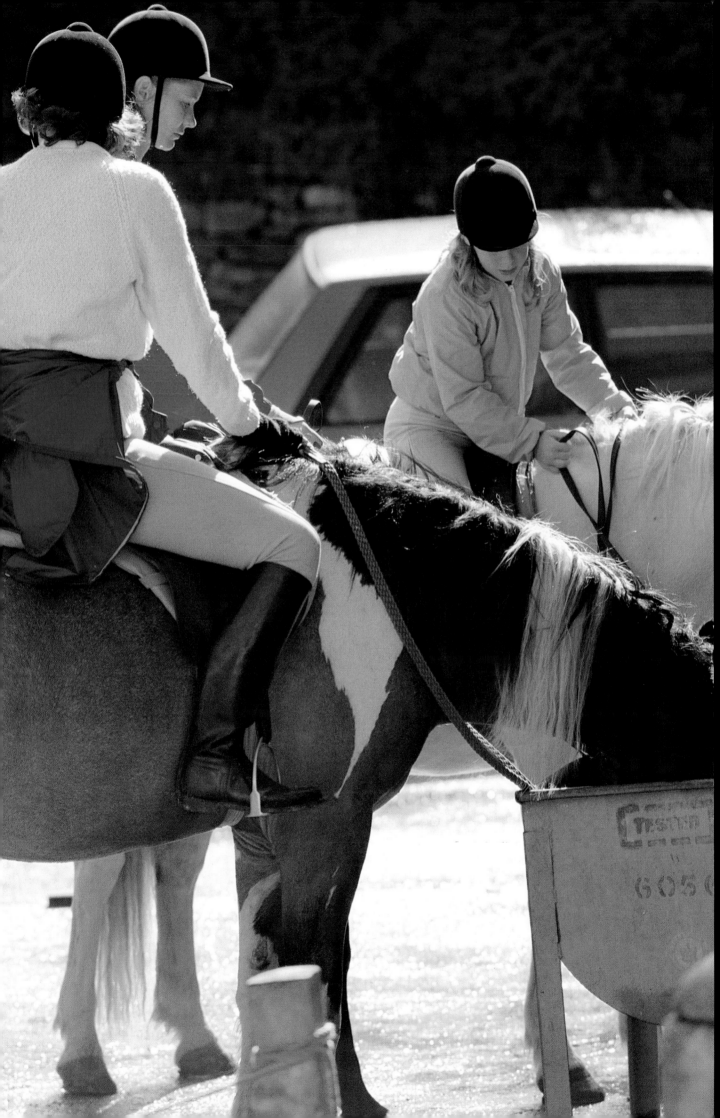

6 First aid

First aid 1: be prepared

One of the great pleasures of riding is going out for the day with a friend, or in a group, to explore the countryside, and to take in the fresh air. Something going wrong is the last thought likely to be on your mind.

Don't panic!

Unfortunately, accidents can happen when out riding and you should know what to do in an emergency. It's easy to panic when faced with an injured person for the first time. But if you are prepared, and are clear about what to do if someone falls off, you should be confident enough to quell your nerves.

Planning is part of the fun of a day out, and your plans should include a scheme for reaching help in case you need it. If you are going quite a way from home, *always* tell someone what route you are taking before you set off, and about what time you expect to arrive back.

▼ **Going out** for a day's ride is great fun, and ponies enjoy new routes too. But the day could end unhappily if you are unprepared to cope with an accident.

Cutting down risks

All ponies can behave unpredictably, particularly in heavy traffic or when startled. But you can reduce the risk of accidents by considerate riding, particularly in a group with beginners. If you are leading the group, don't suddenly go off at a gallop as it can make the ponies at the back of the ride jumpy and eager to follow, and this could unnerve their inexperienced riders.

Whether you are in a group, or just riding with a friend, set the pace to suit the least experienced rider. Like this, no-one gets frightened, and an accident is less likely to happen.

You also need to think about the riding conditions. Be cautious if you try new areas, because the footing may be uneven. Avoid mist and fog, and aim to get home before dusk – your pony is more likely to stumble and fall at the end of the day when he is tired. Above all, steer clear of busy roads.

▲ **If you fall off** and still feel dizzy or in pain, it may be best to walk the pony home rather than get back on and risk another incident.

THE PONIES
If no-one has been badly hurt, turn your attention to the ponies. A pony loose on a road is very dangerous.

If you are already holding one pony, lead him up to the loose one. The free pony is likely to follow. If a pony is loose on his own, try to arouse his curiosity, for example, by rustling something in your hand. When you catch the pony, slowly take hold of the reins – don't grab, or he may be frightened and just run away again.

Are they all right?

When a rider does fall off, a quick glance usually tells you if the damage is serious. The person may be unhurt, but just a little shaken. In this case, catch the pony if it has broken loose, and let your friend sit quietly for a few minutes until feeling well enough to remount. If they are still feeling shaken, head for home, taking the shortest route, and ride back at a quiet pace.

However, if your friend is lying still, or appears to be in pain, the injury is more serious and needs attention.

In a group

When you are in a group, stop the ride. Get someone to hold your pony while you dismount and go to help the hurt rider. Someone else can go and catch the fallen rider's pony if necessary.

While you give the injured person first aid, other riders can go for help if it's needed. They can either telephone for an ambulance, or go to the nearest house to raise the alarm.

Whoever goes for help should make sure they remember the location exactly, otherwise the rescue could be delayed for a long time.

Two of you

Riding on your own, in a place with no passers-by, *you* must assess whether it is necessary to go for help.

Dismount, and tie up your pony. Remember, your own safety is most important; it would help no-one if you were hurt too. For example, don't dash across a road to your friend without first checking it's safe to cross!

Assess and assist

Once at your friend's side, you must assess how bad the injury is. If the casualty is lying still, check the breathing. Someone who is unconscious must *not* be left alone in case their condition becomes worse; stay with the person to make sure their breathing continues without difficulty.

Attract attention by calling loudly or blowing your whistle. If there is no-one around, stay calm. Your home base should realize something is wrong when you do not return on time, and will start looking for you on the route you told them you were taking.

If the casualty is well enough to be left alone – but not to get home – you can go to get help. Before you leave, ensure your friend is protected from passing traffic and from the weather. Again, make sure you can lead rescuers to the exact spot.

Tying up your pony

Once you realize that your friend needs help, quit your stirrups, cross them over while still in the saddle to save time, then dismount and tie up your pony. Ideally you should have brought a headcollar with you on your day out but, on shorter rides, carry in your pocket some breakable twine – not strong nylon baler twine.

Remember the golden rule and never tie up a horse by the bit: don't use the reins to tie him up, or clip a lead-rein to the bit to do so. If the pony jerks his head back, he could hurt his mouth quite badly in the process.

When you use twine, tie it to the noseband, then tie the other end to something secure. If you are in a field, tie your pony to the gate or to a fence post. Near roads, tie him up as far as possible from traffic. Don't leave the reins dangling or the pony may trip on them. Secure them by wedging them under the crossed stirrups or by knotting them.

Your first-aid kit

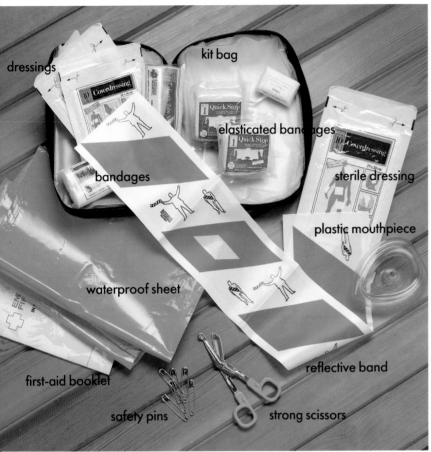

dressings

kit bag

bandages

elasticated bandages

sterile dressing

plastic mouthpiece

waterproof sheet

reflective band

first-aid booklet

safety pins

strong scissors

Taking a first-aid kit with you need not interfere with enjoying your ride out. Well-designed kits are not bulky, and most are the size of a lunchbox — about 25cm × 15cm (10in × 6in). A typical kit contains a wide selection of bandages, including some elasticated ones that offer support and ideally some triangular ones.

You can use dressings of different sizes to cover a wound till you get home, and wear a reflective sash to alert oncoming drivers. Alternatively, you can wave it if you need to attract the attention of passers-by.

A plastic mouthpiece gives added hygiene should you need to give the injured rider the kiss of life. But you need to be taught how it is used in advance.

When it comes to cutting dressings for cuts or grazes you may need a strong pair of scissors. Safety pins help secure bandages.

A waterproof sheet shields the injured person from the rain and damp ground while they wait for help to arrive.

Good first-aid kits also include a small booklet that explains basic treatment.

Other equipment to take

A small back pack is useful for carrying your sandwiches, but leave some room in it for a few other essentials!

One of the items to pack is a clean handkerchief: apart from wiping dirt (or tears!) away, you can use it to stop bleeding, or to remove mud from a companion's eye.

For your pony's safety, carry a hoof pick: you can buy foldaway ones that are light and safe enough to be carried in your pocket. Packing a whistle is sensible too, should you need to attract help. Take a coin for a telephone call, in case you need to contact home: be sure you know the number and area code. Wearing a reflective sash helps rescuers find you more easily in the dark or fog.

To carry all these essential items comfortably, wrap them in a heat-reflective blanket, packing it down to the size of a bar of soap. This prevents a nasty bruise if you are the one to fall off.

The blanket keeps the injured person warm and dry; being wet makes you feel more miserable, and cold can make pain even more intense.

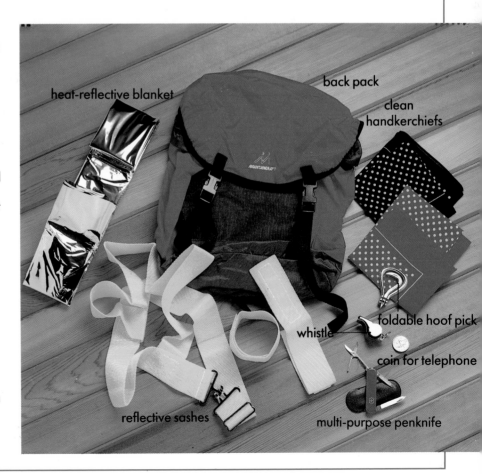

heat-reflective blanket

back pack

clean handkerchiefs

whistle

foldable hoof pick

coin for telephone

reflective sashes

multi-purpose penknife

First aid 2: breathing problems

A sudden mishap to a friend while you're out riding can catch you off guard. Knowing what to do makes it much less frightening. In an emergency, there is an order of steps to take which could help save someone's life: the simplest way to remember these is to think of the letters A B C.

The letter 'A'

'A' stands for Airway. This is the route through the nose and mouth which takes air to the lungs.

A is also for Assistance – if there is any at hand. A helper could telephone for an ambulance, or, when the fallen rider is shaken but not hurt badly, a helper could hold the ponies.

The letter 'B'

B is for Breathing, which is essential to life. A rider who falls and doesn't start to move immediately is either badly winded, in severe pain or – more dangerously – unconscious. You must assess how badly hurt the rider is. Does she respond when you ask if she is all right? Is she still breathing? Or is her breathing noisy, sounding like snoring, which suggests her airway may be partly blocked? If she is lying still, she could well be unconscious.

The unconscious state

Unconscious riders are exposed to danger because they are not aware of their surroundings. They cannot move out of the way of approaching traffic, for example. The person also cannot move to clear their mouth and throat of anything that gets in the way of breathing. The ability to cough – which protects the lungs – goes, and, to make matters worse, the tongue drops limply to the back of the mouth, closing the gap through which air can pass to the lungs. The rider could choke to death.

If the airway is blocked, fresh oxygen cannot reach the lungs to be circulated into the bloodstream, and to get to the brain and the rest of the body. There is an added danger for the unconscious rider lying on their back: fluid from the stomach could flow up into the mouth and spill down into the lungs.

◄ **Knowing** what to do if your friend is hurt could save her life. If she doesn't answer you, get to her side immediately.

▲ **Look to see** that it is safe to get to your friend: it helps no-one if you get hurt too. Quit your stirrups, and cross them while still in the saddle to save time. Cross the right stirrup over first, so when you come to remount, the near one is ready for you to pull down. Dismount and tie up your pony. If you can, tuck the reins under the stirrup irons to stop the pony tripping on them. Leave your friend's pony for the moment; the main point is to get to your friend.

Tie up your pony with breakable twine if you have not taken a headcollar. You can carry the twine in your pocket.

REMEMBER YOUR ABC
To remember the three important steps in saving someone's life think A B C.
☐ **A** is for Airway, the passage for air through the nose and mouth which takes oxygen to the lungs. This has to be kept completely clear at all times.
☐ **B** is for Breathing. Your skill in helping an unconscious rider with breathing difficulties makes all the difference to their chances of rapid recovery.
☐ **C** is for Circulation of the blood. There are steps you can take to help an injured rider who may be bleeding.
☐ **C** also stands for the reCovery position, a position in which a breathing – but unconscious – rider must be placed.

Emergency procedures

1 Get to the injured rider's side as soon as you can, kneel by them and ask loudly and in a clear voice 'Are you all right?' You may need to shake them gently by the shoulder to reinforce the question. If there is little or no response, you must proceed to the next stage: and check first their **A**irway and then their **B**reathing.

2 There are several ways to check that someone is breathing. First, put your cheek close to the injured rider's mouth and nose. Can you feel the warmth of their breath?

If you're not sure, keep your head in the same position and look down the injured rider's body toward their feet. See if their chest is rising and falling.

Giving the kiss of life

Very often, simply correcting the airway (as shown in Figure 1 on the right) is enough to get them breathing again. But if after doing this, they are still not breathing, you must act quickly and give them the kiss of life. Generally, a person can survive for no more than two minutes without breathing, before the lack of oxygen causes brain damage, and deterioration of the body's other vital organs. So you can see why it is important to act quickly!

1 If there is no breathing, or the injured rider is having problem and their breathing is noisy (as if they are snoring), you must correct the **A**irway at once. Put your two fore-fingers on the point of the jaw — not fleshy part. Holding the forehead ar down, lift the jaw upward and forwa

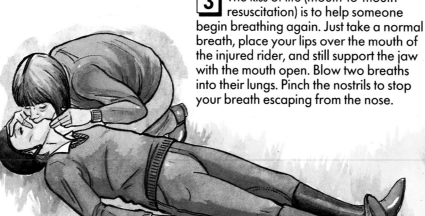

3 The kiss of life (mouth-to-mouth resuscitation) is to help someone begin breathing again. Just take a normal breath, place your lips over the mouth of the injured rider, and still support the jaw with the mouth open. Blow two breaths into their lungs. Pinch the nostrils to stop your breath escaping from the nose.

3 If they are not breathing, you must quickly get air into their lungs again. Undo the chin strap, leaving the hat on, in case they have a neck injury.

4 To start their breathing again, you may have to give them the kiss of life, then loosen their neck clothing, so there is nothing tight around their windpipe.

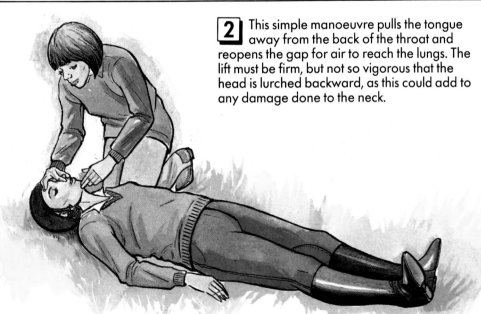

2 This simple manoeuvre pulls the tongue away from the back of the throat and reopens the gap for air to reach the lungs. The lift must be firm, but not so vigorous that the head is lurched backward, as this could add to any damage done to the neck.

4 Give one breath every five seconds — it should be an ordinary breath, not an extra vigorous one. Relax in between breaths. At the same time, count the five-second intervals to yourself, still holding the jaw up. Check that the chest is rising: this means air has entered the lungs.

If you do not see the chest rise with each breath, then either you have not opened the airway fully, or there is an obstruction in the mouth. You can clear this by sweeping the mouth with your finger and gently drawing out any object. Take care not to make the victim sick and not to push the obstruction backward down the throat.

First aid 3: emergency care

▲ An incised cut.

▲ A lacerated cut.

▲ A puncture.
Only scratches and small cuts can be treated by yourself. Any deep cut should be seen by a doctor.

By remembering the first aid ABC in your treatment of an injured rider, you can be sure of getting the priorities right. So, having checked that the Airway is clear and Breathing is regular, you can consider C – Circulation of the blood and the reCovery position for an unconscious person.

Loss of blood

Even a small scratch can damage the body's blood vessels and so lead to bleeding. The body has its own means of trying to protect itself in order to maintain an adequate blood flow. This means that as long as the injury is only a minor one, the body can produce clots to plug the vessel.

With more serious wounds the blood flow is much greater of course, and without the appropriate medical action, the casualty may suffer shock from severe blood loss. It is therefore important to act quickly if someone is losing a large amount of blood.

Direct pressure

Most cuts can best be dealt with by putting pressure directly on the injury. Cover the cut with a sterile dressing or rolled-up handkerchief and press firmly on it with your fingers or thumb. As long as they are able to, you can ask the injured person to apply this pressure for themselves.

Raising the injured area (for example, an arm or leg) also helps to slow down blood flow, but only do this if you are confident it does not hurt the casualty.

Hold the dressing in place and allow

Applying indirect pressure

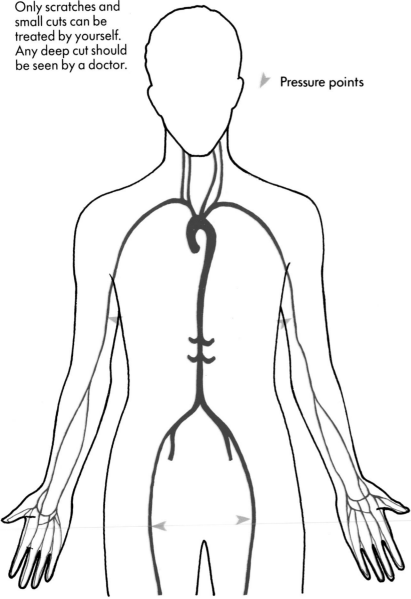

Pressure points

Very occasionally an arm or leg wound bleeds so badly that it cannot be dealt with by applying direct pressure. In such cases – *and only as a last resort* – you can stop the blood flow at a particular pressure point to be found in each arm or in each leg.

The first point lies on the inside of the upper arm and, by pressing upward and inward against the bone, you cut off the blood supply to the whole arm.

The second point lies in the groin on the inside of the thigh. Pressing firmly against the bone here cuts off the blood supply to the leg.

In both cases, the entire limb is affected and pressure should never be maintained for more than 15 minutes. If the bleeding continues, however, release the pressure for a short time before reapplying.

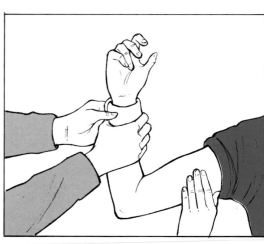

▲ **Indirect pressure** on one of the key pressure points helps to stem heavy bleeding. It should only be used as a last resort – when direct pressure fails – and never for more than 15 minutes. The casualty may be able to help.

5-15 minutes for the bleeding to stop. If blood loss continues, you can use more padding on top of the first layer. Do not remove the original dressing as this may open up the wound again.

In a situation where something is embedded in the cut – a piece of glass, for instance – do not try to remove it. Instead, press firmly alongside the wound and keep gentle but even pressure on its edges.

Nose bleeds

Nose bleeds nearly always come from the soft, fleshy part of the nose. To stop the blood, apply pressure on this part and press below the bone not on it.

Provided there are no other injuries, the casualty can do this quite easily for themselves. Sit them comfortably and tell them to pinch the end of their nose between finger and thumb. They should breathe through the mouth. Make sure the head is forward so that blood does not trickle down the throat and make breathing more difficult. Allow 10 minutes or more to stop the bleeding.

Internal bleeding

Bleeding inside is dangerous because it cannot be seen and symptoms can vary a lot. Generally, you should suspect internal bleeding if the rider has fallen very heavily or if the horse has fallen on top of them. In such cases, the person should be taken to hospital quickly.

If you have to wait long before help comes, avoid moving the casualty. Try to make sure that the head is kept low and loosen any tight clothing such as a tie or belt. Even if they complain of thirst, make sure they do not eat or drink anything. Check the pulse at frequent intervals and pass this information on when help arrives.

Checking the pulse

The pulse is caused by blood moving through the blood vessels as the heart pumps. It is most often checked on the wrist, in line with the bottom of the thumb. Using your fingertips, press gently against the underlying bone. Do not use your thumb as it also has a pulse.

Check whether the pulse is strong or weak, and if it has a steady or irregular rhythm, and count the beats per minute. A normal pulse rate varies, but is most often between 60 and 80 beats a minute.

▲ Direct pressure helps stem bleeding.

▲ Allow 10 minutes for a nose bleed to stop.

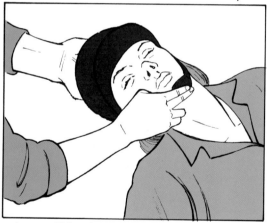

▲ Internal bleeding cannot be seen.

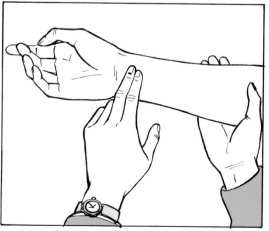

▲ Check the pulse with your fingertips.

REMEMBER YOUR ABC

To remember the three important steps in saving someone's life think **A B C.**

☐ **A** is for **A**irway, the passage for air through the nose and mouth which takes oxygen to the lungs. This has to be kept completely clear at all times.

☐ **B** is for **B**reathing. Your skill in helping an unconscious rider with breathing difficulties makes all the difference to their chances of rapid recovery.

☐ **C** is for **C**irculation of the blood. There are steps you can take to help an injured rider who may be bleeding.

☐ **C** also stands for the re**C**overy position, a position in which a breathing – but unconscious – rider must be placed.

197

GETTING HELP

When you have to stay with an injured person you cannot go to get help. This is where the whistle in a good first-aid kit comes into its own.

Use the whistle to attract attention – and make sure anyone going for help knows what has happened and exactly where the casualty is.

 FIRST-AID CLASSES

The chapters on first aid can only give an introduction to emergency care. It is important that anyone who goes riding often has a good basic understanding of what to do when things go wrong. Find out about first-aid classes near you and take a proper course taught by qualified instructors.

WEARING GLASSES

If an injured person wears glasses, it is always best to remove them and put them somewhere safe until the casualty recovers.

Winding

When someone falls or is hit in the stomach it can knock the air out of their lungs and make it difficult for them to breathe normally. Sit them in a comfortable position and loosen any tight clothing if you are sure they have not hurt their neck or back. It may help to massage gently the top of the stomach – just below the ribs.

The recovery position

As well as Circulation of the blood, **C** stands for the reCovery position for someone who is breathing normally but is unconscious. It is an important part of first aid because it helps to keep the airway open.

Make sure that as you turn the unconscious rider into the recovery position their head and neck move in the same direction as the body. The head must also move at the same *time* as the body. If you have someone with you, get them to help. They can hold the person's neck and head so that it does not turn, fall back, forward or sideways.

The recovery position is only temporary and a person should never be left unattended. Stay with the rider and make sure that their breathing continues without difficulty. Readjust the airway if necessary and be prepared to give reassurance when the person recovers consciousness.

The recovery position

1 Kneel beside the unconscious rider. Place the arm nearest to you above the rider's head – so that she looks like someone in the back crawl swimming position.

3 Hold the rider's head steady and make sure it is supported on her outstretched arm.
   Pull the rider toward you, grasping clothing at the waist or hips. You may be able to use the knee as a lever.

Checking for unconsciousness

When someone falls or gets a bump on the head, they may be confused and dazed but otherwise seem quite healthy. You can gauge their condition by asking simple questions like 'What happened?' or 'What is your name?' If the answers are muddled or make no sense, or if there is any sign of loss of memory, seek medical advice as soon as possible.

A partly or fully unconscious person can drift from one state to another – by recovering or by getting worse. So it is very important to keep a check on the casualty and to watch for any changes that may occur. The depth of

someone's unconsciousness is measured by their response to questions and to gentle contact. If there is no reaction, try pinching the back of their hand. This should prompt them to respond. If they don't, the casualty is deeply unconscious and needs help urgently.

Pinching the back of a person's hand is a bit painful and should prompt a reaction.

Monitoring levels of unconsciousness

When someone loses consciousness, check their eyes, their ability to move and their speech:

Slightly dazed: The person moves when asked and answers questions easily.

Semi-conscious: The casualty may move only in response to pain and open eyes only when asked to. Answers to questions may be confused or make no sense at all.

Deeply unconscious: No reponse to conversation or command. The person cannot move or speak.

Recognizing concussion

A concussed person may briefly lose consciousness.

A blow on the head can often lead to concussion ('brain-shaking'). Typically, the casualty repeats the same question many times, not remembering the answer. Seek medical advice promptly.

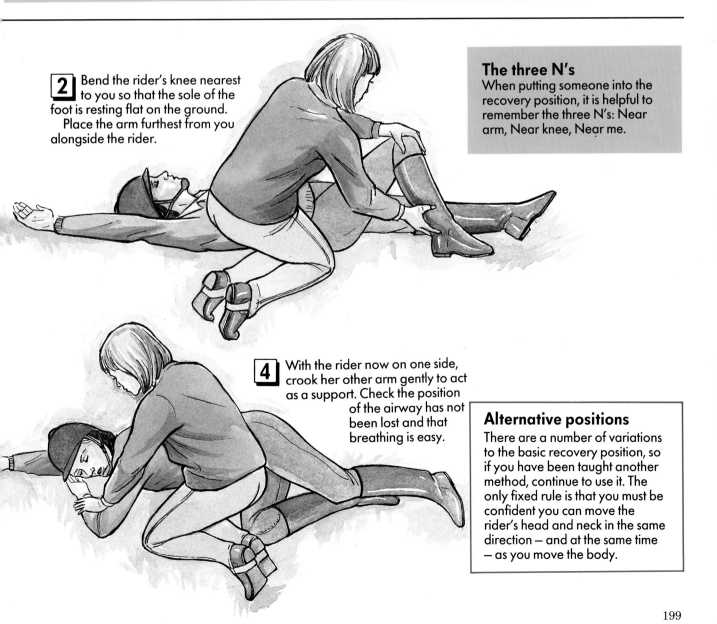

2 Bend the rider's knee nearest to you so that the sole of the foot is resting flat on the ground. Place the arm furthest from you alongside the rider.

The three N's
When putting someone into the recovery position, it is helpful to remember the three N's: Near arm, Near knee, Near me.

4 With the rider now on one side, crook her other arm gently to act as a support. Check the position of the airway has not been lost and that breathing is easy.

Alternative positions
There are a number of variations to the basic recovery position, so if you have been taught another method, continue to use it. The only fixed rule is that you must be confident you can move the rider's head and neck in the same direction – and at the same time – as you move the body.

First aid 4: shock and injury

In an accident, a rider may well suffer from the same kind of injuries as a motorcyclist. Both are likely to be thrown forward from their sitting position – with their heads and arms taking the brunt of the force. What is more, the speed or height of the fall makes for a more serious injury and can, at the very least, leave the rider in a severe state of emotional shock.

Shock treatment

When someone has an accident – especially something sudden like falling off a horse – they may be a bit bruised but otherwise unhurt. However, the surprise and upset caused by the tumble may leave them badly shaken and unwilling to continue riding for a while. In such cases, patience and plenty of reassurance are the best treatment.

Never bully someone into getting back on to the horse until they themselves are ready. It's a complete myth that you lose your nerve if you don't remount after a fall: you are far more likely to develop a dislike for riding if you try to carry on when you are not well. You are also unlikely to be in proper control of your horse – and may have another accident as a result!

After a more serious accident, the combination of pain and injury may cause the rider to go into a state of shock. Blood pressure drops and the body tries to compensate by diverting its blood supply from less important areas (like skin) to vital organs like the brain and heart. Because of this, the casualty looks very pale and often becomes giddy or faints.

A deep state of shock requires urgent medical attention. Try not to move the casualty, but make sure they are kept lying down. As long as it does not hurt them, raise the legs slightly to help circulation. Loosen tight clothing and cover them with the heat-reflective blanket.

While you are waiting for help to arrive, keep a check on their breathing rate and level of consciousness to make sure these do not deteriorate to the point where you have to give mouth-to-mouth resuscitation or put the casualty into the recovery position.

Fractures and dislocations

Before you let a thrown rider remount, you must know how to recognize potentially serious injuries. Apart from problems like difficult breathing, bad cuts and concussion, look for fractured bones and dislocated joints.

A fracture is most likely to be of the collar bone and a dislocation is most often of the shoulder. Both these conditions are painful and the rider will probably realize something is wrong. Gently feel the part that is causing pain and, if it feels or looks different from the normal side, assume it is damaged. If the rider can't move that part of the body without pain – and trying to move makes the pain worse – then you can be pretty sure that they have a fractured bone. You should know how to handle fractures.

Dealing with fractures

The treatment of a fracture is straightforward: leave the injury alone. Make every attempt to prevent the painful part from being disturbed or moved and

★ EMERGENCY PHONE CALLS

When you telephone for help after an accident you should ask for the ambulance service. Once you are put through, be prepared to give the control officer who answers your call the following information:

☐ Your telephone number – in case you are cut off. The control officer can then call you back.
☐ The location of the accident. If it is in open countryside, try to give any useful landmarks.
☐ A description of what happened, including the fact that this was a riding accident.
☐ Whether the casualty is male or female and their approximate age.

Do not hang up first: let the control officer complete the call. This way you can be sure he has all the information needed. You can then return to the site of the accident, as the control officer will contact any other emergency services that may be required.

◄ **If, after a bad accident,** the casualty becomes pale and their skin feels cold and clammy, they are probably in a state of shock. This is a serious condition which requires urgent medical attention.
► **While waiting** for help, do not move the casualty unless it is essential. Keep them warm and, as long as it does not hurt them, raise the legs a little to help their circulation.

let the casualty stay still as much as possible. Keep them warm and watch for symptoms of shock setting in.

Supporting a fracture – with slings and padding – is the task of a trained first aider who knows how to use bandages and splints but you must take action in certain situations. If the rider is complaining of pain in the neck or back, for example, make sure they do *not* try to sit up or stand up as they may well have neck or spine injuries.

You must also get help quickly when someone has broken a large bone such as the thigh bone. These injuries are easy to identify as the damaged limb looks deformed and is painful. Less obvious is the danger of internal bleeding, which can only be dealt with at a hospital. The casualty is likely to suffer

Checking for injury

1 Do not remove the riding hat in case the neck is injured. Keep the casualty still and ask if they feel tenderness or pain anywhere along their spine.

2 Feel the collar bones and shoulders. Loosen tight clothing round the neck and see if the casualty has a medallion indicating the need for special treatment.

DISLOCATIONS
When a bone is jolted out of position at a joint, it is very painful and quite alarming as the dislocation often looks badly deformed.

Do not touch the injured area but sit the casualty down as comfortably as possible. Arrange for them to be taken to hospital as soon as possible.

5 Using both hands at the same time, examine the hips, thighs, knees, lower legs, ankles and feet. This way, it is easier to notice differences on one side of the body compared with the other.

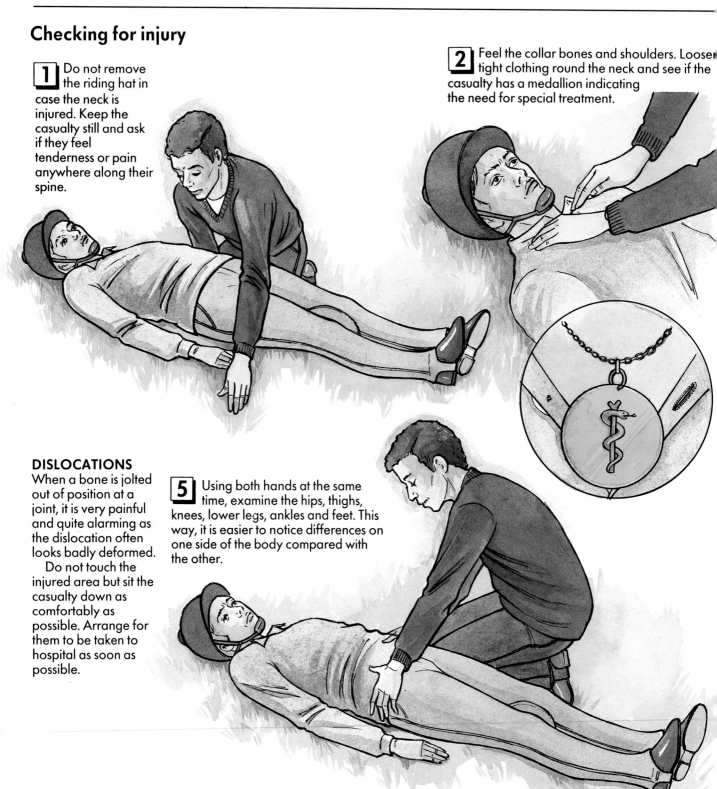

from shock so do what you can to reassure them, see they are not left alone and get help urgently.

Checking for injury

When checking someone who has had an accident, remember the basic ABC and first make sure that their breathing is normal and that they are not bleeding badly. Avoid moving them unless it is absolutely necessary.

Begin by checking the head and neck for injury, then work carefully down to the feet. Look at both sides of the body to see if one is out of shape compared with the other – a clue to dislocation or fractures. Do not forget to examine the wrists and ankles as well as arms and legs, as these joints are very prone to injury.

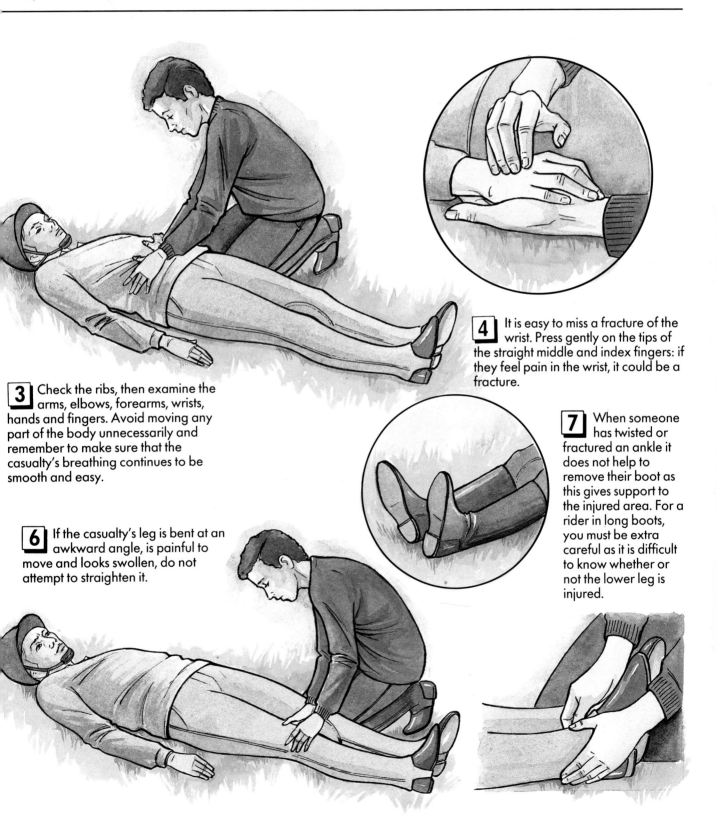

4 It is easy to miss a fracture of the wrist. Press gently on the tips of the straight middle and index fingers: if they feel pain in the wrist, it could be a fracture.

3 Check the ribs, then examine the arms, elbows, forearms, wrists, hands and fingers. Avoid moving any part of the body unnecessarily and remember to make sure that the casualty's breathing continues to be smooth and easy.

7 When someone has twisted or fractured an ankle it does not help to remove their boot as this gives support to the injured area. For a rider in long boots, you must be extra careful as it is difficult to know whether or not the lower leg is injured.

6 If the casualty's leg is bent at an awkward angle, is painful to move and looks swollen, do not attempt to straighten it.

First aid 5: minor injuries

Knowing the appropriate first aid after major accidents is an important skill for all serious riders to have. But, surprisingly often, your know-how is needed for treating much less dramatic problems.

Scratches and scrapes

Although such injuries are not serious, they should be kept as clean as possible to avoid the risk of future infection. For very small scratches, a strip of adhesive dressing should give enough protection. Larger scrapes can be covered with a pad of sterile dressing held in place with plasters or a bandage.

A speck in the eye

Riding at speed, in the company of others, can easily lead to dust or grit flying up into the eyes, making it difficult to see. If the problem persists, you can usually remove the irritation with the corner of a handkerchief.

When it is difficult to locate what is causing the problem, ask the casualty to sit or kneel down. Stand behind them and hold their eyelids apart with your index finger and thumb. Ask them to look up, down, right and left so that you can see into the affected eye more thoroughly.

If you cannot remove the irritant, or if it is stuck to the coloured part of the eye, you must seek medical aid.

Insect stings

Being stung by an insect such as a bee, wasp or horsefly is painful and upsetting rather than dangerous. The best way to ease the pain is by applying a cold compress to the swollen area.

If someone is stung in the mouth, give them sips of cold water to rinse over the swelling. Make sure their breathing does not become difficult — perhaps because the sting has made the tongue swell up and obstruct the airway. In such cases, hospital treatment may be necessary.

Blisters

Painful little blisters are often caused by silly mistakes such as tight boots or the reins rubbing against the fingers. In such cases — where it's difficult to stop the cause — the best solution is to cover the swollen area with an adhesive dressing large enough to go well beyond the edges of the blister itself.

! TETANUS WARNING

Always ask an injured person when they last had an anti-tetanus injection — especially if they have been cut or bitten by an animal.

Tetanus (lockjaw) is a potentially fatal disease so most school children are automatically given the necessary course of inoculations. However, boosters are needed throughout adult life and the dates they were given are very important.

STING IN THE TAIL

When someone is stung by a bee, the sting often remains in their skin. If you can see it sticking out, gently remove it with a pair of tweezers. Do not try squeezing it out with your fingers as this simply spreads the irritant poison more quickly into the skin.

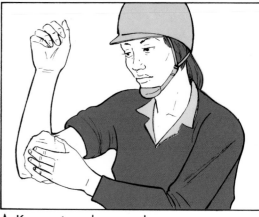

▲ Keep cuts and grazes clean.

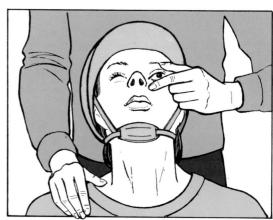

▲ Stand behind when checking the eye.

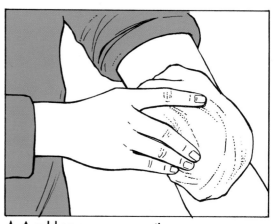

▲ A cold compress eases stings.

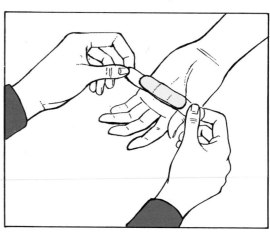

▲ Put an adhesive dressing on blisters.

Heat-stroke

In very hot weather, the body sometimes finds it difficult to maintain the correct temperature and the results can be serious. If someone complains of a dizzy headache and looks either uncomfortably flushed or very pale, give them immediate attention.

The most important thing is to help them cool down. Move them into a shady place, remove their riding hat and any heavy clothing and give them sips of water to drink. If the casualty does not recover quickly, send for medical help.

Minor burns

When someone gets burnt – either by a bit too much sun or by something like a rope being pulled suddenly through their hands – your immediate aim should be to cool the affected area. Apply a cold-water compress or running water to the burn and allow at least 10 minutes for it to be effective. A sunburnt person may also be suffering from general exposure to heat: in such cases, treat them as if they had heat-stroke. Anyone with severe burns needs urgent hospital attention, so get help fast.

▲ A cold drink helps in hot weather.

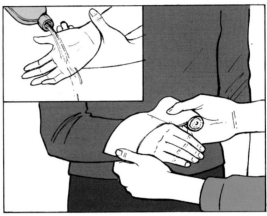
▲ Minor burns can be cooled with water.

THINK AHEAD
Even quite small burns can quickly cause the skin to swell. Before this happens, gently loosen any tight clothing around the burnt area.

Also check to see if the casualty is wearing anything like a watch or ring which might become uncomfortably tight.

Action checklist summary

☐ Make sure that there is no immediate danger to yourself or to the casualty. If there are several of you, see that someone takes care of the injured rider's pony as soon as possible.

☐ Remember the first-aid ABC and treat the casualty in order of priority: airway, breathing, circulation, recovery position.

☐ Do not leave an injured person alone: keep an eye on them until help arrives and be prepared to deal with changes in their condition.

☐ Do not move the casualty unless it is essential.

☐ After a heavy fall, be aware that the rider may have internal injuries. Do not give them anything to eat or drink.

► Remember that prevention is better than cure: wear the correct riding gear, let people know where you are going and always keep to the level of the most inexperienced rider. Stay clear of busy roads whenever you can.

Index

ACKNOWLEDGEMENTS

Photographs: Animal Photography 182-3; Bruce Coleman (Eric Crichton) 118; Martin E Dalby 121(t); Kit Houghton 121(b), 130-1, 132(tl), 141(br), 143, 144-9, 150-1, 153(t), 156, 164, 175, 176(b), 177, 180(r), 185; Lamtec Ltd 76(l); Bob Langrish 49, 54, 80-1, 84-5, 96-7, 98-9, 101(b), 102, 110, 112, 114(bc), 152, 154, 160-1, 165, 176(tr); Only Horses Picture Library 64-5; Peter Roberts Collection 162(b), 171; Spectrum 170, 184; John Suett/Eaglemoss 191; Steve Tanner/ Eaglemoss 89(b); TSW 178-9; Elisabeth Weiland 132(tr); ZEFA 174, 181.
All other photographs: Shona Wood.

Illustrations: Catherine Constable 9, 10-11; Michael Cooke 54-5; Coral Mula 27, 103, 139, 166, 173; Denys Ovenden 63, 74-5, 77; Maggie Raynor 12-13, 16-17, 21, 24, 28-9, 33, 36-7, 38-9(b), 50-1, 55(c), 106-7, 110, 130-1, 152, 157, 194-5, 196-9, 202-5.